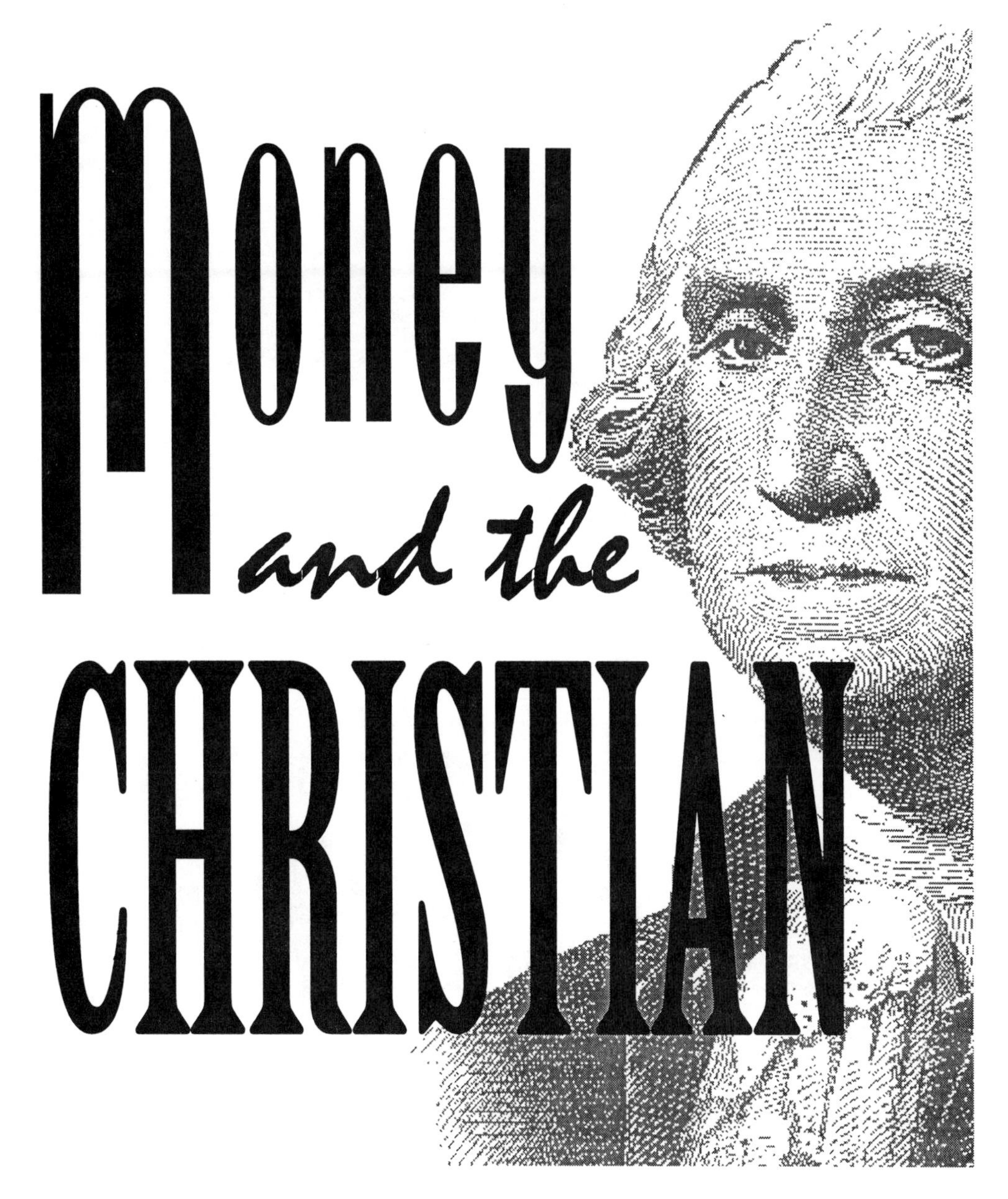

A Course in Biblical Economics

by

Caleb McAfee

Caleb McAfee Ministries • P.O. Box 153989 • Irving, Texas 75015-3989

For information about how your church can sponsor a
Money and the Christian Seminar,
write or call:

Caleb McAfee
P.O. Box 153989
Irving, Texas 75015
(972) 438 1234

ISBN #0-9656010-0-5

The use of italics or underlining in the Scripture portions is done so at the discretion of Caleb McAfee to emphasize a certain word or thought.

Scriptures, unless otherwise noted, are from the New International Version (New York International Bible Society,1978)

Other Scriptures as notes are from:
TLB, The Living Bible, Paraphrased (Wheaton, Tyndale House, 1971)
Phillips, The New Testament in Modern English (J.B. Phillips, Macmillan Company, 1958)
Williams, The New Testament: A Translation in the Language of the People (Moody Bible Institute, 1937, 1965)
The New English Bible (Oxford University Press and Cambridge University Press, 1961)

Acknowledgments

Thousands of years ago Solomon wrote, "There is nothing new under the sun." (Ecclesiastes 1:9) My philosophy of biblical economics has been influenced by the many excellent books I have read on the subject and by the mentors God has brought into my life.

Special, special thanks to Mary, my devoted and loving wife. She believes in the calling God has placed on my life. She is the joy of my life. Like the wisdom she brings, "nothing can compare with her." (Proverbs 8:11) She has selflessly spent many hours in the creation and formatting of what you hold in your hand. Without her counsel and many contributions to the seminar, this book and the seminar would not exist.

Thanks to our many friends and relatives who loyally stand with us and serve as a source of inspiration and encouragement.

Special thanks to my friend, Paul Mills, who first urged me to develop the seminar, to my pastor, Tom Wilson, who undergirds this ministry with prayer, to DeVern Fromke whose counsel I value and seek often and to J. Don George whose encouragement and advice has proven invaluable.

Special thanks and appreciation to Kathie Grice, our Office Manager, who for many years has served tirelessly behind the scenes doing whatever is needed to make things run smoothly.

Also thanks to Pamella May. No person is more devoted to this ministry than our enthusiastic, energetic Director of Scheduling.

Above all, thanks to my boss, the Chief Executive Officer and Chairman of the Board of the ministry, God Himself, who is the source and reason behind it all.

TABLE OF CONTENTS

CHAPTER 1

CHAPTER 2

CHAPTER 3

CHAPTER 4

CHAPTER 5

CHAPTER 6

CHAPTER 7

CHAPTER 8

CHAPTER 9

INTRODUCTION

WELCOME

Welcome to this course in biblical economics. During our time together you will discover what God has to say about your finances. His Word has established clear-cut principles for sound money management; principles that, when applied in faith, will insure success and financial freedom for you and your family. His way works!

A COURSE FOR ALL CHRISTIANS

This course is designed both for those who are successful in financial management who want to learn how to be more successful by following godly principles and for those who find themselves in financial difficulties and want help.

FOR THOSE IN FINANCIAL STRAITS

If your financial situation is less than ideal, before you proceed with this course of study, do the following:

1. **Don't despair.**

   Besides being sinful, worry and anxiety do not provide the atmosphere of faith and hope needed to produce your financial breakthrough.

2. **Turn to the Lord in a time of crisis.**

   At this time avoid mentally trying to calculate a way out of your financial problems. Instead allow the Holy Spirit to minister hope to your spirit.

Psalm 27:14

Wait for the Lord; be strong and take heart and wait for the Lord.

Psalm 46:1

God is our refuge and strength, an ever-present help in trouble.

3. Seek the Lord earnestly.

He is not trying to avoid you. He promises to be easily found by those who are serious about seeking him and his ways.

Jeremiah 29:11-13

"For I know the plans I have for you," declares the Lord, "plans to prosper you and not to harm you, plans to give you hope and a future. Then you will call upon me and come and pray to me, and I will listen to you. You will seek me and find me when you seek me with all your heart. I will be found by you."

4. Believe that God will rescue you as his Word is received and acted upon in faith.

Isaiah 46:4

I am he who will sustain you. I have made you and I will carry you; I will sustain you and I will rescue you.

5. Carefully read and meditate every scripture in the right hand columns.

This book is not always written in prose form but is designed as a study guide.

Romans 10:17 (KJV)

Faith cometh by hearing and hearing by the Word of God.

6. Determine to learn from your experience so you can minister to others who are experiencing your same situation.

II Corinthians 1:3,4

Praise be to God...the Father of compassion and the God of all comfort who comforts us in all our troubles, so that we can comfort those in any trouble with the comfort we ourselves have received from God.

CHAPTER 1

Three Definitions to Insure That We Are on the Same Wavelength

You must be careful to reject the world's narrow definition of the following three words. By clarifying in your mind what they truly mean, you will be better prepared to pursue them as belonging to you by birthright.

Prosperity — (Proverbs 13:21 NIV)

1. Having more than enough to do what God has called you to do
2. Walking in an understanding of *El Shaddai* (literally translated, "all-bountiful, the God of more than enough")

Success — (Joshua 1:8 KJV)

1. The progressive realization of God-given goals
2. Discovering and fulfilling God's purpose for your life

Financial Freedom — (John 8:36)

1. Choosing to serve God rather than money
2. A life of faith and contentment free from financial worries
3. Knowing that God is in control

THREE THINGS THIS COURSE CAN ACCOMPLISH FOR YOU

1. MAKE YOU ELIGIBLE FOR TRUE RICHES

To the degree you can responsibly handle financial matters, God deems you trustworthy to handle spiritual matters.

The same principles used for accurate bookkeeping are the principles used to gain spiritual wisdom. Since Solomon asked for wisdom instead of money, God could give him both. (I Kings 3:12,13)

Luke 16:11

So if you have not been trustworthy in handling worldly wealth, who will trust you with true riches?

2. MAKE YOU AN EFFECTIVE SERVANT OF GOD

God does not want you emotionally tied up in knots over financial worries. Financial bondage limits a Christian's effectiveness as a servant of the Lord in his or her earthly walk. Many fear the future. Fear is the reciprocal of faith. It gives Satan a free hand to continue destroying your financial future.

Matthew 13:22

The one who received the seed that fell among the thorns is the man who hears the word, but the worries of this life and the deceitfulness of wealth choke it, making it unfruitful.

Luke 8:50

Don't be afraid; just believe.

The word *worry* is derived from an old Anglo-Saxon word meaning "to choke."

a. Worry chokes emotionally.

b. Worry frustrates.

c. Worry affects health.

d. Worry neutralizes the power of faith.

Philippians 4:6

Do not be anxious about anything.

The key to escape the worry habit and slavery to money is to *decide* to serve God rather than money.

Matthew 6:24

No one can serve two masters. Either he will hate the one and love the other, or he will be devoted to the one and despise the other. You cannot serve both God and Money.

3. GIVE YOU FREEDOM

• *Freedom From Debt*

(Debt is when your assets are less than your liabilities.)

1. Debt makes you a servant to the lender.
2. Debt presumes upon the future.
3. Debt hinders giving.
4. Debt hinders ministry.
5. Debt erodes resources through high interest payments.
6. Debt promotes impulse buying.

• *Freedom From the Love of Money*

(building your life around money)

Romans 13:8

Keep out of debt altogether, except that perpetual debt of love which we owe one another.

Proverbs 22:7

The rich rule over the poor and the borrower is servant to the lender.

James 4:13-15

Now then you who say, "Today or tomorrow we will go to this or that city, spend a year there, carry on business and make money." Why, you do not even know what will happen tomorrow...instead you ought to say, "If it is the Lord's will, we will live and do this or that."

Luke 14:18-20

But they all alike began to make excuses. The first said, "I have just bought a field..." Another said, "I have just bought five yoke of oxen..."

I Timothy 3:3-5

...not a lover of money. He must manage his own family well...(if any-one does not know how to manage his own family, how can he take care of God's church?)

The love of money:

- ☐ Makes you ineligible for church leadership
- ☐ Is the source of most evil
- ☐ Leads astray
- ☐ Brings many griefs

• *Freedom From Financial Pressure*

(fear of unexpected expenses when every dollar is needed for past and present obligations)

1. Financial pressure causes you to live a life of fear as opposed to one of faith.
2. Financial freedom comes as a result of understanding the Kingdom of God and applying its principles in our daily lives.

• *Freedom From Business Entanglements*

(allowing your business to crowd out the more important things)

I Timothy 6:10

For the love of money is a root of all kinds of evil. Some people, eager for money, have wandered from the faith and pierced themselves with many griefs.

Proverbs 10:22

The blessing of the Lord brings wealth, and he adds no trouble to it.

Matthew 6:25-34

Therefore I tell you, do not worry about your life, what you will eat or drink; or about your body, what you will wear...for the pagans run after these things, and your heavenly Father knows that you need them. But seek first his kingdom and his righteousness and all these things will be given to you as well.

Matthew 13:18-23

Listen then to what the parable of the sower means: When anyone hears the message about the kingdom and does not understand it, the evil one comes and snatches away what was sown in his heart. This is the seed sown along the path. What was sown on rocky places is the man who hears

1. Involvement vs. entanglement

2. Allowing business to crowd out the Word, prayer and family

3. Working the job around the family

4. Proper priority:

   a. God

   b. Family

   c. Business or job

• *Freedom From the Desire to Get Rich, Especially to Get Rich Quick*

(looking for ways to make large amounts of money without commensurate labor)

the Word and at once receives it with joy. But since he has no root, he lasts only a short time. When trouble or persecution comes because of the Word, he quickly falls away. What was sown among the thorns is the man who hears the Word, *but the worries of this life and the deceitfulness of wealth choke it,* making it unfruitful. But what was sown on good soil is the man who hears the Word and understands it. He produces a crop, yielding a hundred, sixty or thirty times what was sown.

II Timothy 2:3,4

Endure hardship with us like a good soldier of Christ Jesus. No one serving as a soldier gets involved in civilian affairs. He wants to please his commanding officer.

I Timothy 6:9,10

People who want to get rich fall into temptation and a trap and into many foolish and harmful desires that plunge men into ruin and destruction ...flee these things.

Proverbs 28:22 (KJV)

He that hasteth to be rich hath an evil eye, and considereth not that poverty shall come upon him.

Proverbs 23:4

Do not wear yourself out to get riches; have the wisdom to show restraint.

FOUR STEPS TO REALIZE FINANCIAL FREEDOM

Step One:

Deliverance

The spirit of poverty in your personal finances can be broken by the delivering power of Christ, the Anointed One and his anointing.

Poverty vs. "being broke"

1. Poverty is a spiritual mind-set; whereas "being broke" may be a temporary condition not involving the spirit of poverty.

2. Poverty is a part of the curse from which we have been redeemed.
 (See Deuteronomy 28)

Luke 4:18

The spirit of the Lord is on me because he has anointed me to preach good news to the poor. He has sent me to proclaim freedom for the prisoners and recovery of sight for the blind, to release the oppressed, to proclaim the year of the Lord's favor.

Galatians 3:13

Christ redeemed us from the curse of the law by being a curse for us.

II Corinthians 8:9

For you know the grace of our Lord Jesus Christ, that though he was rich yet for your sakes he became poor so that you through his poverty might become rich.

I John 3:8

The reason the Son of God appeared was to destroy the devil's work.

John 10:10

The thief comes only to steal and kill and destroy; I have come that they may have life, and have it to the full.

Step Two:

A Proper Attitude Toward God—Faith

To experience financial freedom, an accurate understanding of the loving, caring nature of our Father God is imperative. You cannot rise above your conception of God.

Some people see God as an angry God just waiting for them to step out of line. But…

A. God loves you—He wants to bless you.

B. God wants you to succeed—He wants to prosper you.

C. God has a wonderful plan for your life.

III John 2 (KJV)

Beloved, I wish above all things that thou mayest prosper and be in good health even as thy soul prospereth.

Psalm 35:27

The Lord be exalted who delights in the prosperity of his servant.

Isaiah 48:17,18 (KJV)

I am the Lord your God who teacheth thee to profit, which leadeth thee by the way thou shouldest go.

Job 36:11

If they obey and serve him they will spend the rest of their days in prosperity and their years in pleasure.

Deuteronomy 8:18

But remember the Lord your God, for it is he who gives you the ability to produce wealth, and so confirms his covenant.

Jeremiah 29:11

"For I know the plans I have for you," declares the Lord, "plans to prosper you and not to harm you, plans to give you hope and a future."

Step Three:

A Proper Attitude Toward Self

You cannot love others until you learn to love yourself, until you have proper self-esteem. For the believer, healthy self-esteem is seeing yourself as God sees you.

You are unique:

- Created in the image of God
- Heir of God and co-heir with Jesus
- Son of God

Change what you can and, aside from the work of the enemy which you should relentlessly resist, accept the rest.

Choose to be happy regardless of your circumstances.

Matthew 22:37-39

Jesus replied: "'Love the Lord your God with all your heart and with all your soul and with all your mind.' This is the first and greatest commandment. And the second is like it: 'Love your neighbor *as* yourself.' All the Law and the Prophets hang on these two commandments."

Romans 8:16-17

The Spirit himself testifies with our spirit that we are God's children. Now if we are children, then we are heirs—heirs of God and co-heirs with Christ, if indeed we share in his sufferings in order that we may also share in his glory.

I John 3:2

Beloved, now are we the sons of God...

Step Four:

A Change in Behavior

For lasting results after deliverance, there must be an accompanying change in:

your attitude — mentality

your life-style— conduct

your thinking—“renewing of the mind”

Romans 12:2

Be transformed by the renewing of your mind.

Romans 12:2 (Phillips Translation)

Don’t let the world around you squeeze you into its own mold, but let God remold your minds from within, so that you may prove in practice that the plan of God for you is good, meets all his demands and moves toward the goals of true maturity.

Ephesians 4:17

So I tell you this, and insist on it in the Lord, that you must no longer live as the Gentiles do, in the futility of their thinking.

These Scriptural laws, with their accompanying promises, only work when applied.

Joshua 1:8

Do not let this Book of the Law depart from your mouth; meditate on it day and night so that you may be careful to do everything written in it. *Then* you will be prosperous and successful.

There are serious consequences for failing to do what the Word says. The Book of Deuteronomy calls these consequences, "curses."

Deuteronomy 28:15,29

However, if you do not obey the Lord your God and do not *carefully follow* all his commands and decrees I am giving you today, all these curses will come upon you and overtake you...You will be unsuccessful in everything you do; day after day you will be oppressed and robbed, with no one to rescue you.

Hosea 4:6

My people are destroyed from lack of knowledge.

Two conditions that hinder God's blessing:

1. Lack of knowledge

2. Lack of diligence

John 8:31,32

Jesus said, "If you *hold to* my teaching, you are really my disciples. *Then* you will know the truth, and the truth will set you free."

James 1:22-25

Do not merely listen to the Word, and so deceive yourselves. *Do what it says.* Anyone who listens to the Word but does not do what it says is like a man who looks at his face in a mirror and, after looking at himself goes away and immediately forgets what he looks like. But the man who looks intently into the perfect law that gives freedom and continues to do this, not forgetting what he has heard, but doing it—he will be blessed in what he does.

CHAPTER 2

STEWARDSHIP

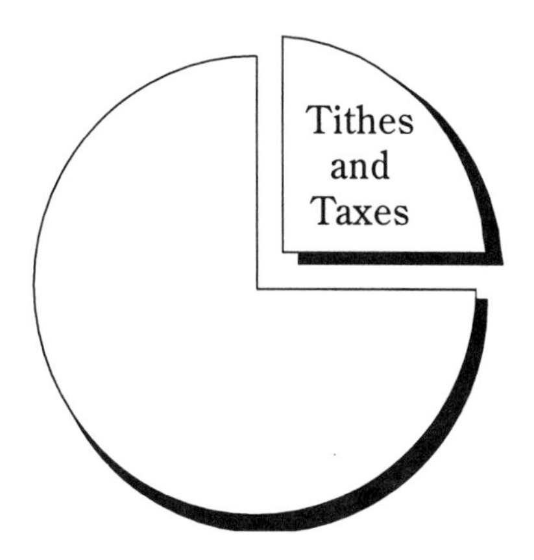

Quiz*

After paying tithes and taxes, you are free to use the remainder anyway that is moral, legal and ethical.

☐ True

☐ False

Definition of Stewardship

- The dictionary defines a steward as one who is charged with the responsibility to manage the property of another. He or she is a fiscal agent charged with the collection and disbursement of funds. Ron Blue defines stewardship as, "the use of God-given resources for the accomplishment of God-given goals."

- In contemporary language, the word "stewardship" can be translated as management or administrative oversight and the word "steward" can be translated as a manager, trustee or administrator.

  Stewardship is foundational to an understanding of biblical financial freedom.

*For the answer, see page 23.

Before we proceed into this important study, first take some time to fill out the "Net Worth Statement" on the following page.

NET WORTH STATEMENT

Where you are financially?

Date: ______________

ASSETS:

Cash on hand (currency, checking accounts, etc.)	______
Savings (money markets, credit union, savings accounts)	______
Cash value of life insurance	______
Investments	
Stocks owned	______
Bonds owned	______
Value in profit-sharing or pension plan	______
Real estate	______
Personal dwelling	______
Investment property(s)	______
Household furniture	______
Automobiles (current book value)	______
Personal property	
Wardrobe	______
Recreational equipment	______
Yard equipment	______
Jewelry	______
Business inventory	______
Special items (cameras, collections, electronics, etc.)	______
Other	______

TOTAL ASSETS: ______________

LIABILITIES:	Int. Rate	Payment	Balance
Home mortgage	____	____	______
Other mortgage(s)	____	____	______
Loans	____	____	______
Bank	____	____	______
Finance company	____	____	______
Credit union	____	____	______
Credit cards	____	____	______
Car loans	____	____	______
Personal loans	____	____	______
Judgments	____	____	______
Other obligations	____	____	______
	____	____	______

TOTAL LIABILITIES: ______________

NET WORTH: (assets less liabilities) ______________*

* The value of the assets over which you have been appointed a steward

1. GOD OWNS EVERYTHING

- If God owns everything, then it is only reasonable that he has the right to whatever he wants, whenever he wants.

Psalm 24:1

The earth is the Lord's and everything in it, the world and all who live in it.

- It is all his.

Haggai 2:8

"The silver is mine and the gold is mine," declares the Lord Almighty.

- How you use *his* resources becomes a spiritual decision.

- Your checkbook "tells all" about how serious you are concerning stewardship.

Psalm 50:7-12

For every animal of the forest is mine, and the cattle on a thousand hills. I know every bird in the mountains and the creatures of the field are mine...for the world is mine, and all that is in it.

WHERE DOES WEALTH ORIGINATE?

David's prayer over the gifts offered for the building of the temple clearly identifies the source of wealth.

I Chronicles 29:10-14

David praised the Lord in the presence of the whole assembly saying: "...for everything in heaven and earth is yours. Yours, O Lord, is the kingdom. You are exalted as head over all. Wealth

- The Bible warns against boastfully taking credit for the attainment of your own possessions.

- God gives the ability, ideas and anointing to produce wealth.

- Wealth enables you to fulfill the covenant—to be a blessing. (See Genesis 12:2)

YOU CANNOT TURN OWNERSHIP OVER TO GOD. IT IS ALREADY HIS.

- Not only your possessions, but *YOU* belong to him.

  Stewardship involves far more than just monetary concerns.

- You belong to him by virtue of the fact that he made you.

and honor come from you...but who am I, and who are my people that we should be able to give as generously as this? Everything comes from you, and we have given you only what comes from your hand."

Deuteronomy 8:17,18

You may say to yourself, "My power and the strength of my hands have produced this wealth for me." But remember the Lord your God, for it is he who gives you the ability to produce wealth, and so confirms his covenant which he swore to your forefathers, as it is today.

Romans 12:1

Therefore, I urge you, brothers, in view of God's mercy, to offer your bodies as living sacrifices, holy and pleasing to God—which is your spiritual worship. (KJV—"reasonable service")

Psalm 100:3

Know that the Lord is God. It is he who made us, and we are his; we are his people, the sheep of his pasture.

- Furthermore, you belong to him by virtue of the fact that he redeemed you with the blood of Jesus.

I Corinthians 6:19,20

Do you not know that your body is a temple of the Holy Spirit, who is in you, whom you have received from God? *You are not your own; you were bought at a price.* Therefore honor God with your body.

I Peter 1:18

For you know that it was not with perishable things such as silver or gold that you were redeemed from the empty way of life handed down to you from your forefathers, but with the precious blood of Christ.

- Whenever you call Jesus "Lord" you are really acknowledging his ownership.

  Gk: *kurios* translated "lord" means owner, controller or authority

Philippians 2:10,11

That at the name of Jesus every knee should bow, in heaven and on earth and under the earth, and every tongue confess that Jesus Christ is LORD, to the glory of God the Father.

- Everything has its origin and purpose in Jesus Christ.

Colossians 1:16

For *by* him all things were created: things in heaven and on earth, visible and invisible, whether thrones or powers or rulers or authorities; all things were created *by* him and *for* him.

2. GOD HAS DEFERRED MANAGEMENT OF WHAT YOU POSSESS INTO YOUR HANDS

YOU POSSESS, BUT GOD OWNS

- You manage the Lord's property as his asset manager.

In essence, you act as his agent.

When you do anything in his name, it is like having the power of attorney to act as his agent and do on his behalf what he would do.

Furthermore, he owns you and all you possess, but defers the management to you. This is stewardship.

I Corinthians 4:7

What do you have that you did not receive?

Proverbs 27:23

Be sure you know the condition of your flocks, give special attention to your herds.

YOU BECOME A TRUSTEE

The total of all your possessions and yourself is the current inventory of your trust account. This trust account is to be administered by you, as the trustee of the beneficiary, God himself.

You are responsible to be a good manager. Beyond that you are free. You are free from the tyranny of things.

Before God will add to the trust account, he is watching for trustworthiness in little things before he entrusts you with greater things.

I Corinthians 4:2

Now it is required that those who have been given a trust must prove *faithful*.

Luke 16:10,12

Whoever can be trusted with very little can also be trusted with much, and whoever is dishonest with very little will also be dishonest with much. *And if you have not been trustworthy with someone else's property, who will give you property of your own?*

Some examples of irresponsible management of your trust account:

☐ **Impulse buying**

- Buying without first seeking the Lord's approval
- Buying without first checking quality
- Buying without first conducting a price comparison

☐ **Neglect of the trust property**

- Not exercising preventative maintenance

☐ **Carelessness in details**

- Inattention to where money goes
- Living beyond your means

When a trustee uses the inventory for his or her own gratification, this trustee is guilty of fraud and embezzlement. He or she is guilty of the sin of greed.

Proverbs 24:30-34

I went past the field of the sluggard, past the vineyard of the man who lacks judgment; thorns had come up everywhere, the ground was covered with weeds, and the stone wall was in ruins. I applied my heart to what I observed and learned a lesson from what I saw: a little sleep, a little slumber, a little folding of the hands to rest and poverty will come on you like a bandit and scarcity like an armed man.

GREED IS THE OPPOSITE OF STEWARDSHIP

- It is part of the earthly nature to be possessive and to never be satisfied. Greed is a work of the flesh that must be conquered.

  Greed is a translation of the Greek word *pleonexia*.

  This word is made up of the following two Greek words:

  pleon—more
  echo—to have
  It literally means, a desire to have more.

Colossians 3:5-8

Put to death, therefore, whatever belongs to your earthly nature: sexual immorality, impurity, lust, evil desires and greed which is idolatry...you used to walk in these ways, in the life you once lived. But now you must rid yourself of all such things.

- It angers God.

Isaiah 57:17

I was enraged by his sinful greed.

- Greed is so sinful that Christians are instructed to not even associate with the greedy.

I Corinthians 5:11

But now I am writing you that you must not associate with anyone who calls himself a brother...but is greedy. With such a man do not even eat.

- Consider what greed is associated with in the scripture.

Ephesians 5:3,5-7

But among you there must not be even a hint of sexual immorality or of any kind of impurity or of greed, because these are improper for God's holy people. For of this you can be sure: No immoral, impure or greedy person—such a man is an idolater—has any inheritance in the kingdom of Christ and of God. Let no one deceive you with empty words, for because of such things God's wrath comes on those who are disobedient. Therefore do not be partners with them.

- A man of God must not be greedy.

Exodus 18:21

But select capable men from all the people—men who fear God, trustworthy men who hate dishonest gain—and appoint them as officials.

- Jesus warns to be on guard against greed.

Luke 12:15

Then He said to them, "Watch out! Be on your guard against all kinds of greed; a man's life does not consist in the abundance of his possessions.

The following is a **prayer of relinquishment.** If you can sincerely pray this prayer, indicate by dating and signing below:

Dear Heavenly Father,

I acknowledge your ownership of me and everything I have. I cannot transfer anything to you. I can only acknowledge that I possess in trust, but you own. I hereby acknowledge my stewardship responsibilities and purpose to be found faithful in the discharge of my duties.

I know that some day I will give an accounting of how I have administered your property. My greatest goal is to hear the words from your lips, "Well done, good and faithful servant! You have been faithful with a few things; I will put you in charge of many things. Come and share your master's happiness!" (Matthew 25:21)

I now renew my commitment to seek your kingdom first and foremost. I pray this prayer in Jesus' name. Amen.

____________________ Signed   ____________ Date

____________________ Signed   ____________ Date

* The correct answer to the Quiz on page 15 is false. If Jesus is not the Lord of all, then he is not Lord at all. You must involve his Lordship over everything he has entrusted to your oversight. There are no discretionary funds exempt from stewardship.

CHAPTER 3

LEARN THE FINE ART OF CONTENTMENT

CONTENTMENT IS AN ATTITUDE

- Contentment does not depend upon what you have.
- Success is not a destination. It is an enjoyable journey.

  You can be just as happy today as when you totally fulfill your goal.

  Don't allow circumstances to control your attitude.

  If you don't have what you like, then like what you have until you attain what God has inspired you to believe for.

- A frenzied striving spirit portends poverty.
- A confident attitude of contentment paves the road to success.
- Spiritual rest and contentment produces gain—great gain.
- The dictionary defines *discontentment* as a dislike of what one has and a desire for something different; feeling not satisfied; uneasiness; restlessness.

Luke 12:15

A man's life does not consist in the abundance of his possessions.

II Corinthians 6:10

Sorrowful, yet always rejoicing; poor, yet making many rich; having nothing, and yet possessing everything.

I Timothy 6:6-8

But *godliness with contentment is great gain.* For we brought nothing into the world, and we can take nothing out of it. But if we have food and clothing, we will be content with that.

- Material possessions in and of themselves do not bring contentment.

"I wish" summarizes where most people live. They never enjoy the present.

Learn to "neutralize" the influences of the world which are designed to weaken your self-worth and create a lack of satisfaction:

Television
Catalogs
Shopping

Bill Gothard defines *contentment* as "realizing that God has provided everything I need for my present circumstances." I add to his definition, "And the ability to enjoy it."

Hebrews 13:5

Keep your lives free from the love of money and *be content with what you have,* because God has said, "Never will I leave you; never will I forsake you."

CONTENTMENT VS. COMPLACENCY

Contentment is a spiritual rest.

Complacency is a fatalistic acceptance of the *status quo.*

- You must *LEARN* to be content
- The secret of contentment is *seeing Christ as our supply.*

Philippians 4:11-13

I am not saying this because I am in need, for *I have learned to be content* whatever the circumstances. I know what it is to be in need, and I know what it is to have plenty. *I have learned the secret of being content in any and every situation,* whether living well-fed or hungry, whether living in plenty or in want. I can do everything through him who gives me the strength.

SOME PRACTICAL STEPS LEADING TO CONTENTMENT

Learn to:

- ☐ Reduce living expenses below income.
- ☐ Place value on what you have, not on what you want.
- ☐ Express appreciation for things you usually take for granted.
- ☐ Get pleasure in protecting the possessions entrusted to you.

Proverbs 21:20 (TLB)

The wise man saves for the future, but the foolish man spends whatever he gets.

I Thessalonians 5:16,18

Be joyful always; give thanks *in* all circumstances.

Luke 16:10-12

Whoever can be trusted with very little can also be trusted with much, and whoever is dishonest with very little will also be dishonest with much. So if you have not been trustworthy in handling worldly wealth, who will trust you with true riches? And if you have not been trustworthy with someone else's property, who will give you property of your own? No servant can serve two masters.

LEARN THE TRUE VALUE OF MONEY

CHILDREN MUST BE PREPARED FOR THE REAL WORLD OF FINANCE

- In our society you don't get anything for free.
- If you work you should expect to benefit.
- If a child learns that industry brings reward and laziness brings difficulties, he or she will have taken a major step toward being a financial success as an adult.

LEARN TO RELATE THE COST OF AN ITEM TO THE TIME EXPENDED TO ACQUIRE IT

- You give up some of your time in exchange for money.

Proverbs 22:6-7

Train a child in the way he should go, and when he is old he will not turn from it. The rich rule over the poor, and the borrower is servant to the lender.

I Corinthians 9:10

When the plowman plows and the thresher threshes, they ought to do so in *the hope of sharing in the harvest.*

Romans 4:4

Now when a man works, his wages are not credited to him as a gift, but as an obligation.

Proverbs 20:4

A sluggard does not plant in season; so at harvest time he looks but finds nothing.

- You use the money in exchange for commodities another person has exchanged his or her time to produce or acquire.

- Paying cash can help you realize the true cost of an asset or service.

LEARN TO TRULY "EARN" THE MONEY YOU GET

- Work is a requirement and a privilege.

- Work is so important that it was the first thing God gave man to do.

- In addition to supplying your physical needs, work supplies seed, a sense of identity and self-worth, an opportunity to practice spiritual principles and a platform to represent God in this world.

Genesis 3:19

By the sweat of your brow you will eat your food until you return to the ground, since from it you were taken; for dust you are and to dust you will return.

II Thessalonians 3:10

If a man will not work, he shall not eat.

Genesis 2:15

The Lord God took the man and put him in the Garden of Eden to work it and take care of it.

PRAYERFULLY SET A GOAL TO EXCEL PROFESSIONALLY AND INCREASE YOUR EARNING CAPACITY

- To earn more at your job you must become more valuable. You must qualify for more money.
- Faithful service is rewarded. Ultimately your income should match your service.
- People who do just enough to get by or only what they are paid for should never expect pay increases or advancements.

  —the idea of trying to get something for nothing does not work.

> **KEY TRUTH**
> **The more you do of what you are now doing, the more you will have of what you've got. For things to change, you must change.**

SOME INCOME-ENHANCING STEPS

1. Develop the habit of focused thinking.

Each morning spend 15 minutes contemplating such questions as:

How can I effectively increase my service and become a more profitable employee today?

Matthew 25:23,29

Well done, good and faithful servant! You have been faithful with a few things; I will put you in charge of many things. For everyone who has will be given more, and he will have an abundance.

Luke 12:42-44

The Lord answered, "Who then is the faithful and wise manager, whom the master puts in charge of his servants to give them their food allowance at the proper time? It will be good for that servant whom the master finds doing so when he returns. I tell you the truth, he will put him in charge of all his possessions."

Mark 10:43

Whoever wants to become great among you must be your servant.

What results are expected of me?

What can I do that will make a difference in my company's success?

What part can I play in increasing profits and decreasing losses?

Why am I on the payroll?

2. **At an appropriate time after you have demonstrated that you are a "profitable servant," respectfully ask the person who makes the decisions about your career:**

    What steps must I take in order to become more valuable to you and our company and therefore increase my earning potential?

3. **Develop the "proprietary instinct."**

    Reject the "us against them" (labor against management) attitude prevalent in the work force.

4. **Study and emulate successful people.**

    Make sure that your role models are winners. Relationships determine what you will become.

5. **Always remember for whom you are really working.**

- Visualize the Lord inspecting your work.

Ecclesiastes 10:10

If the ax is dull and its edge unsharpened, more strength is needed, but skill will bring success.

Proverbs 22:29

Do you see a man skilled in his work? He will serve before kings; he will not serve before obscure men.

Luke 16:13

You cannot serve both God and money.

II Timothy 2:15

Do your best to present yourself to God as one approved, a workman who does not need to be ashamed.

Proverbs 13:20

He who walks with the wise grows wise, but a companion of fools suffers harm.

Colossians 3:22-24

...Obey your earthly masters in everything; and do it, not only when their eye is on you and to win their favor, but with sincerity of heart and reverence for the Lord. *Whatever you do, work at it with all your heart, as working for the Lord, not for men,* since you know that you will receive an inheritance from the Lord as a reward. It is the Lord Christ you are serving.

Ephesians 6:5-8

...obey your earthly masters with respect and fear... Serve wholeheartedly as if you were serving the Lord, not men, because *you know that the Lord will reward everyone for whatever good he does...*

- By faith believe that God will give advancement.

Psalm 75:6 (KJV)

Promotion cometh neither from the east, nor from the west nor from the south.

6. Believe for the Lord's blessing, not only on yourself, but on the company for whom you work because of you.

- In order for God to bless and prosper you, he may have to bless and prosper your employer.
- Start an idea file and expect God to help you fill it with creative ideas for you and your company.

Genesis 39:2-5

The Lord was with Joseph and he prospered, and he lived in the house of his Egyptian master. When his master saw that the Lord was with him and that the Lord gave him success in everything he did, Joseph found favor in his eyes and became his attendant. Potiphar put him in charge of his household, and he entrusted to his care everything he owned. From the time he put him in charge of his household and of all that he owned, the Lord blessed the household of the Egyptian because of Joseph. The blessing of the Lord was on everything Potiphar had, both in the house and in the field.

7. Guard the Lord's testimony on the job.

Make the Lord attractive by how you represent him. Earn respect.

If your boss does not recognize your contribution, God can see to it that another one does.

II Corinthians 5:20

We are therefore Christ's ambassadors.

I Timothy 6:1

...consider their masters worthy of full respect, so that God's name and our teaching may not be slandered.

Titus 2:9,10

Teach...to be subject to their masters in everything, to try to please them, not to talk back to them, and not to steal from them, but to *show that they can be fully trusted so that in every way they will make the teaching about God our Savior attractive.*

I Peter 2:18,19

...submit yourselves to your masters with all respect not only to those who are good and considerate, but also to those who are harsh...but if you suffer for doing good and you endure it, this is commendable before God.

SOME SPIRITUAL BENEFITS MONEY CAN PRODUCE

Conventional thinking is that money can provide security, establish independence and create power. God has a different purpose for money.

WAYS GOD MAY USE MONEY:

1. To develop trustworthiness

Luke 16:11

So if you have not been trustworthy in handling worldly wealth, who will trust you with true riches?

2. To provide daily needs

Matthew 6:11

Give us this day our daily bread.

3. To confirm the Lord's will and direction
   - It is safe to assume that until God provides funds for an object or a project, that it is probably not his will.
   - A person with unlimited funds or unlimited credit will have more difficulty determining the Lord's will. God gave special warning to the rich.

I Timothy 6:17

Charge them that are rich in this world, that they be not high-minded, nor trust in uncertain riches, but in the living God.

Proverbs 11:28

Whoever trusts in his riches will fall.

4. To demonstrate the Lord's faithfulness to our family and community

Malachi 3:10,12

"Bring the whole tithe into the storehouse, that there may be food in my house. *Test me in this,*" says the Lord Almighty, "and see if I will not throw open the floodgates of heaven and pour out so much blessing that you will not have room enough for it...then all the nations will call you blessed."

5. To multiply the potential for giving

II Corinthians 9:6,10,11

Remember this: Whoever sows sparingly will also reap sparingly, and *whoever sows generously will also reap generously.* Now he who supplies seed to the sower and bread for food will also supply and increase your store of seed and will enlarge the harvest of your righteousness. You will be made rich in every way so that you can be generous on every occasion, and through us your generosity will result in thanksgiving to God.

Don't work just to earn a living.

Ephesians 4:28

He who has been stealing must steal no longer, but must work, doing something useful with his own hands, that he may have something to share with those in need.

6. To lay up treasure in heaven

Matthew 6:19-21

Do not store up for yourselves treasures on earth, where moth and rust destroy and where thieves break in and steal. But store up for yourselves treasures in heaven...for where your treasure is, there your heart will be also.

I Timothy 6:18,19

Command them to do good, to be rich in good deeds and to be generous and willing to share. In this way they will lay up treasure for themselves as a firm foundation for the coming age, so that they may take hold of the life that is truly life.

CHAPTER 4

THE DEBT TRAP

BORROWING HAS BECOME A WAY OF LIFE

- The average American owes in excess of $4,000 in installment credit (not counting home mortgages).
- Payments on mortgage and consumer debts consume nearly three-fourths of the average annual income after taxes.
- Our nation has gradually turned from a cash economy to an all-consuming debt economy, beginning first with financing of the home, then the car, the refrigerator, consumer goods, luxuries and finally even pleasures.

Proverbs 14:12 (TLB)

Before every man there lies a wide and pleasant road that seems right but ends in death.

SLOGANS OF OUR TIME

"Buy now, pay later"—the catch is that you still have to pay and until you do, you have to pay interest.

Most consumer debt bears interest of 15%-21%.

Many families pay over $1,000 per year interest on installment debt thus reducing their future standard of living.

"Instant credit"— this means instant debt.

"Easy payments"— this means, uneasy payments later.

Proverbs 20:25

It is a trap for a man to dedicate something rashly and only later to consider his vows.

Proverbs 13:15

The way of transgressors is hard.

DEBT OUTPACES RAISES

People sink deeper into debt assuming income will increase to cover the payments.

What may have been true in the 70's and early 80's is no longer true now. Today you cannot pay back a loan with "cheaper" dollars caused by a high inflation factor nor is personal interest tax deductible.

EXPANDING DEBT

Many families are oblivious how overwhelming a problem debt can become.

Look at this family who spends only $3.29 a day ($100 per month) more than it earns. Assume an average credit card interest of 18% compounded monthly for 15 years.

Year	Amount Overspent	Accumulated Interest	EOY Balance
1	$1,200	$104	$1,304
2	1,200	463	2,863
3	1,200	1,128	4,728
4	1,200	2,157	6,957
5	1,200	3,621	9,621
6	1,200	5,608	12,808
7	1,200	8,217	16,617
8	1,200	11,572	21,172
9	1,200	15,818	26,618
10	1,200	21,129	33,129
11	1,200	27,714	40,914
12	1,200	35,821	50,221
13	1,200	45,749	61,349
14	1,200	57,855	74,655
15	1,200	72,562	90,562
	$18,000	$72,562	$90,562

The purpose of the previous illustration is to demonstrate how overspending a modest amount each day can wreck a family's finances and become an overwhelming problem. The family illustrated has lost its freedom. Such a course of action would likely have caused this family's finances to self-destruct before the 15 years illustrated.

BEWARE IF YOU HAVE ANY OF THESE WARNING SIGNS OF IMPENDING DOOM

1. One credit card is used to pay another.
2. One bill is delayed so an overdue bill can be paid.
3. Getting a new loan or extension to pay your debt.
4. Paying only the minimum amount due on charge accounts.
5. Using your checking account "overdraft" to pay regular bills.
6. Using credit card cash advances to pay living expenses.
7. Using credit to buy things you used to be able to buy with cash.
8. Using savings to pay bills.
9. Depending on overtime to make ends meet each month.
10. Co-signing a note.

Proverbs 22:7

The rich rule over the poor, and the borrower is a servant to the lender.

Luke 16:13

You cannot serve both God and Money.

Haggai 1:6 (TLB)

Your income disappears, as though you were putting it into pockets filled with holes!

Deuteronomy 6:13-14

Fear the Lord your God, serve him only...Do not follow other gods, the gods of the peoples around you.

Proverbs 6:1-3 (TLB)

If you endorse a note for someone...guaranteeing his debt, you are in serious trouble...Quick! Get out of it if you can.

SEVEN QUESTIONS TO ASK IF MONEY DOES NOT EXIST TO PAY FOR A WANT OR A NEED

- ☐ Is God trying to tell me something?
- ☐ Do I really need it? Right now?
- ☐ Have I misspent the money God has already supplied for it?
- ☐ Will acquiring it increase my effectiveness in serving God?
- ☐ Could it be replaced with a less expensive item?
- ☐ Have I done price comparisons?
- ☐ Have I given God an opportunity to provide it?

EIGHT CONSEQUENCES OF BORROWING

1. **Borrowing consumes resources through interest payments.**

   The cost is higher than most can imagine.

Luke 14:28-30

Suppose one of you wants to build a tower. Will he not first sit down and estimate the cost to see if he has enough money to complete it? For if he lays the foundation and is not able to finish it, everyone who sees it will ridicule him, saying, "This fellow began to build and was not able to finish."

Deuteronomy 28:43-45 (TLB)

While you become poorer and poorer, they shall lend to you, not you to them!...All these curses shall pursue and overtake you until you are destroyed--all because you refuse to listen to the Lord your God.

The following shows the high cost of financing the purchase of a home:

Loan	$85,000
Interest Rate	9%
Term	30 Years
Payments	$683.93
# of Payments	x 360
	$246,215

In 5 years

	$683.93	
	x 60	Payments
	$41,036	

Original Loan	$85,000
Less: Principal Reduction	3,502
New Balance	$81,498

In 10 years

	$683.93	
	x 120	Payments
	$82,072	

Original Loan	$85,000
Less: Principal Reduction	8,985
New Balance	$76,015

In 15 years

	$683.93	
	x 180	Payments
	$123,107	

Original Loan	$85,000
Less: Principal Reduction	17,569
New Balance	$67,431

The following shows the high cost of financing the purchase of a car:

New car cost	$18,000
Monthly payments (10% down, 7%, 48 months)	$387.93
Total paid for car	$20,421
Approximate value of the "used" car in 4 years	$6,350

Assume you purchase and finance a new car every four years over a working life of 40 years, you will have purchased 10 new cars and paid car payments of $186,206.

What if, instead of making car payments, you paid yourself $387.93 per month and were able to invest that payment at 10%, you would have $2,453,300. If you were able to invest at 15% you would have $12,032,058. This is the true cost of buying the new cars, not the total of the payments.

The exhibit on Page 55 entitled "Cost of Car Ownership" at the end of this chapter demonstrates the benefits of buying a well-maintained, low-mileage, three-year-old automobile and driving it for 4 years as opposed to purchasing the same car new and driving it for 4 years.

2. **It denigrates the Lord's reputation.**

   It says to the world: God is not supplying all my needs, therefore I have to make up the slack by borrowing.

3. **It removes the barriers to harmful things.**

   God may be protecting you from harmful things by not providing the money. If you borrow to get it anyway, you in effect, are circumventing the Lord's wisdom.

Malachi 3:18

And you will again see the distinction between the righteous and the wicked, between those who serve God and those who do not.

James 4:3 (KJV)

You ask and receive not, because ye ask amiss that ye may consume it upon your lusts.

4. It fosters impulse buying.

Impulse buying is when decisions are based solely upon the whim of the moment rather than prayerfully considering the decision and allowing God to even, sometimes, supernaturally provide it.

5. It interferes with God's provision.

God has promised to meet the needs of his children. He wants you to put your trust and faith in him, rather than a line of credit.

6. It represses creativity.

There may be an alternate means to obtain the needed

7. It presumes upon the future.

To do so violates Scripture.

Proverbs 21:5

Haste leads to poverty.

I John 2:16 (TLB)

The ambition to buy everything that appeals to you, and the pride that comes from wealth and importance...these are not from God. They are from this evil world itself.

II Chronicles 16:9 (KJV)

For the eyes of the Lord run to and fro throughout the whole earth, to show himself strong in the behalf of them whose heart is perfect toward him.

Matthew 13:44-46

The kingdom of heaven is like treasure hidden in a field. When a man found it, he hid it again, and then in his joy went and sold all he had and bought that field. Again, the kingdom of heaven is like a merchant looking for fine pearls. When he found one of great value, he went away and sold everything he had and bought it.

James 4:13,14

Now listen, you who say, "Today or tomorrow we will go to this or that city, spend a year there, carry on business and make money." Why, you do not even know what will happen tomorrow.

8. It is not the Lord's best.

Borrowing is usually related to God's judgment.

Deuteronomy 28:15,43,44

If you do not obey the Lord your God...the alien who lives among you will rise above you higher and higher, but you will sink lower and lower. ***He will lend to you, but you will not lend to him.*** He will be the head, but you will be the tail.

DEBT IS SYMPTOMATIC OF THE REAL PROBLEM

While debt itself is not a sin, the Bible discourages the use of debt.

Debt is a symptom of the real problem.

The underlying root problem is usually:

- greed
- impatience
- lack of self-discipline
- poor self-image

Once you know the real cause, getting out of debt becomes easier.

STEPS TO GETTING OUT OF DEBT

1. Have a family meeting and prayerfully set a goal to live God's way.

Write the goal down on paper. Make it a visible and objective standard to work toward.

Prayerfully write out a schedule for accomplishment, establishing target dates. Expect an anointing to achieve debt-free living.

Your written goal should cover a workable plan for these three areas:

1. How to stop spending more than you make
2. How to pay the interest on the debt you have accumulated
3. How to repay the debt

See the goal reached with the eyes of faith. By faith, daily affirm something like this: *"We are acknowledging Him and He is directing our paths. We are blessed, and all of our needs are supplied by Christ Jesus. We have given, so I know it is given unto us. It's ours now, even though we do not see it. It belongs to us. We're believing God!"*

2. Start paying the Lord's tithes.

This stops the 20% penalty God collects for failure to pay. (Leviticus 27:30-33—more on this later) Of course, you want the Lord's blessing on your debt reduction plan!

Matthew 18:19,20

If two of you on earth agree about anything you ask for, it will be done for you by my Father in heaven. For where two or three come together in my name, there am I with them.

II Corinthians 9:8

And God is able to make all grace abound to you, so that in all things at all times, having all you need, you will abound in every good work.

Proverbs 21:5

The plans of the diligent lead to profit.

Mark 11:24

Therefore I tell you, whatever you ask for in prayer, believe that you have received it, and it will be yours.

Matthew 23:23 (TLB)

Yes, you should tithe.

Malachi 3:11

I will rebuke the devourer for your sakes.

3. **Add no new debt.**

Do without if that is what it takes.

You may want to keep one or two credit cards which have no annual fee and which offer at least a 25-day grace period before charging interest. These are to be used as a convenience, and all purchases must be paid off within 25 days of purchases thus incurring no interest charge. If you do not have the discipline to use the cards correctly, do not carry them in your wallet or perhaps you may have to even close the accounts. For some, a card destruction ceremony may be appropriate.

4. **Face the facts of your situation.**

Fill out the form entitled "Obligations" on page 59 at the end of this chapter.

5. **Reduce standard of living to allow a monthly debt reduction program.**

Benjamin Franklin said that there are only two ways to solve financial difficulties, "Diminish your wants, or augment your means."

After the payment of fixed expenses, and the cost of the bare necessities, apply all extra income to pay off debt.

Proverbs 14:8

The wisdom of the prudent is to give thought to their ways, but the folly of fools is deception.

Apply any unexpected monies toward debt reduction:

- income tax refund
- inheritance
- pay raise
- overtime
- bonus
- any other additional income

6. Consolidate bills if you can save on interest.

Do not use consolidation to extend debt, only consolidate if you can lower the interest rate.

Be sure and don't add to your debt even if it is offered.

7. Move the outstanding balance on high interest rate cards to cards offering a lower rate.

Choose a card with at least a 25-day grace period with low or no annual fee. When the balance is finally reduced to zero you can continue to use the card and pay for purchases within the grace period.

8. Implement a rapid debt reduction program for high interest rate home mortgages.

Purchase *HOME FREE!* by Caleb McAfee. This program offers step-by-step plans to enable you to pay off your mortgage in half the remaining term or less.

The strategies contained in this package can save you tens of thousands of dollars of mortgage interest.

For purchasing information, see the Order Form in the back of this book.

Isaiah 48:17 (TLB)

"I am the Lord your God who...leads you along the paths that you should follow."

9. Ask the Lord for creative ways to earn extra funds to liquidate debt:

- ☐ Garage sale
- ☐ Consider selling the second car
- ☐ Working mother
  (Analyze the facts first. Fill out the form "Working Mother—Income and Expenses" on page 58 of this chapter.
- ☐ Analyze the equity in your home
- ☐ Money-making projects such as:
  - house cleaning
  - baby-sitting
  - lawn service
  - tutoring
  - consulting
  - painting and household repair
  - starting a small business

10. Learn to barter assets or skills you have for things you need.

To barter, you must find the person who has what you want and is willing to exchange it for what you have.

Examples: You could trade baby-sitting, children's clothing, landscaping, painting, house repairs, car repairs, car pooling, fresh produce, etc., all of which you otherwise would have paid cash for. It's easy and it's lots of fun.

11. Sacrifice a little extra, and get out of debt in half the time.

(See the form entitled "Monthly Payments at 15% Interest" on page 56 of this chapter.)

12. Follow the instructions on page 60 and fill out the "Order of Debt Repayment" form on page 61.

13. Be determined to never give up until you are debt-free.

Never despair. It may have taken years to accumulate the debt. Faithful application of these strategies, coupled with patience and trust will extricate you. Believe God for a way of escape.

Proverbs 3:5,6

Trust in the Lord with all your heart and lean not on your own understanding; in all your ways acknowledge him and he will direct your paths.

Hebrews 6:12

Imitate those who through faith and patience inherit what has been promised.

DEBIT CARDS

If you lack the discipline to control a credit card, if you take literally Romans 13:8, or if you are philosophically opposed to debt in any form, consider a debit card. It is like a plastic check.

1. A debit card looks exactly like a Visa or a MasterCard.

2. It is honored by any merchant who accepts major credit cards.

3. The cost of the purchase is deducted from your interest-bearing account instead of being billed to you each month.

4. It cannot be abused. There is no way to spend more than the amount you have in the account.

5. Other than an annual card fee, there are no credit costs or interest charges.

6. It can be used as a cash substitute for traveler's checks. You can get cash withdrawals without the fees generally imposed on credit card withdrawals.

7. Get a debit card from some banks, savings and loans, or credit unions. The following brokers provide them as a part of their cash management packages:

Kemper	800-231-5142
Charles Schwab	800-421-4488
Fidelity	800-343-8721

8. Guard your debit card carefully. Unlike its credit card cousin, there is no $50 limitation for unauthorized usage. A thief can use the debit card to the extent of your balance.

COST OF CAR OWNERSHIP

New Car vs. Used Car

	New car every 4 years $18,000, 10% down, 7%, 48 months				Same car 3 years old $7,500 cash purchase			
Year	1	2	3	4	1	2	3	4
Gasoline (1)	$1,200	$1,200	$1,200	$1,200	$1,200	$1,200	$1,200	$1,200
Oil	60	60	60	70	70	70	70	70
Maintenance	0	50	250	270	250	270	300	320
Repairs	0	0	0	350	350	500	600	700
License	60	60	60	60	60	60	60	60
Sales tax (6%)	1,140	0	0	0	510	0	0	0
Insurance (2)	770	700	690	635	538	488	272 (5)	272 (5)
Payments	4,655	4,655	4,655	4,655	0	0	0	0
Down payment	1,800	0	0	0	7,500	0	0	0
Opportunity cost (3)	180	180	180	180	750	750	750	750
Depreciation	4,500	3,500	2,500	1,150	1,000	1,000	1,000	1,000
Fund to acquire next car (4)	*	*	*	*	1,000	1,000	1,000	1,000
COST PER YEAR	$14,365	$10,405	$9,533	$8,570	$13,228	$5,338	$5,252	$5,372

(1) Based on 18,000 miles per year, 17 mpg, $1.15/gal.

(2) Based on $100/300/50 coverage, $2,500 PIP, $100 deductible on comprehensive, $200 deductible on collision, $40 towing, rental car reimbursement and $25/50/25 uninsured motorist

(3) Interest (10%) that could have been earned on money spent on car

(4) One-fourth of the amount needed (in 4 years) to make up the difference between the resale value of your car, and the price of the next one you buy (4 years from now). This amount is to be accumulated in an interest-bearing account. For the new car purchase it is assumed that the value of the car at trade in would more than cover the cost of down payment of next new car.

(5) At this point the owner drops the comprehensive and collision and becomes self-insured due to the reduced replacement value of the older car

Four Year Cost of Ownership:

New Car	$42,873
Used Car	29,190
Savings	$13,683

MONTHLY PAYMENTS AT 15% INTEREST

Debt	Year 1	2	3	4	5	6
$1,000	$ 90.26	$ 48.49	$ 34.67	$ 27.83	$ 23.79	$ 21.15
2,000	180.52	96.97	69.33	55.66	47.58	42.29
3,000	270.77	145.46	104.00	83.49	71.37	63.44
4,000	361.03	193.95	138.66	111.32	95.16	84.58
5,000	451.29	242.43	**173.33**	139.15	118.95	**105.73**
6,000	541.55	290.92	207.99	166.98	142.74	126.87
7,000	631.81	339.41	242.66	194.82	166.53	148.02
8,000	722.07	387.89	277.32	222.65	190.32	169.16
9,000	812.32	436.38	311.99	250.48	214.11	190.31
10,000	902.58	484.87	346.65	278.31	237.90	211.45

Monthly payments of $105.73 would liquidate $5,000 of indebtedness in six years. It does not require doubling the monthly payment in order to pay off the total debt in one-half the time.

If $67.60 of principal could be added to the six-year payment amount, the debt would be liquidated in only three years.

Seek God for creative ways to pay more principal which goes directly to debt reduction.

MONTHLY CASH FLOW ANALYSIS

Date: ______________

Gross Monthly Wages ______________

Less: Total Payroll Deductions ______________

Less: Misc. Payroll Deductions ______________

COMBINED TAKE-HOME WAGES $ ____________

Additional Income:

Dividends & Interest ______________

Small Business Income ______________

Pensions/Annuities ______________

Other ______________

Total Additional Income $ ____________

TOTAL MONTHLY INCOME
(combine Take-Home Wages & Total Additional Income) $ ______________

Less Expenses:

The Lord's Tithe ______________

Offerings ______________

Payments on debts *(excluding car and house)* ______________

Mortgage/Rent ______________

Utilities, Etc. ______________

Food ______________

Clothing ______________

Medical *(including insurance)* ______________

Gifts ______________

Transportation *(including car expenses)* ______________

Entertainment/ Recreation ______________

Other Commitments ______________

Total Expenses $ ____________

NET CASH FLOW
(*Total Monthly Income Less Total Expenses)* $ ______________

WORKING MOTHER— INCOME AND EXPENSES

	Hypothetical		Yours	
Gross income per week (40 hrs. @ $6.00/hr.)		$240.00		________
Less: Tithe (10%)	$24.00		________	
Offerings (5%)	12.00		________	
Federal income tax (15%)	36.00		________	
Social Security tax (7.65%)	19.00		________	
Transportation (10 trips of 5 mi. @ 30¢ per mile)	15.00		________	
Child care (1 child)	70.00		________	
Meals/coffee @ $6/day	30.00		________	
Convenience foods at home	20.00		________	
Extra clothing (including cleaning & cosmetics)	6.00		________	
Beauty shop	14.00		________	
Other ("I owe it to myself") items	5.00		________	
Total Expenses		$251.00		________
NET USABLE		$ (11.00)		________

TIME SPENT:		
On the job	40 hours	________
Lunch	5 hours	________
Travel	5 hours	________
Hours away from home	50 hours	________

OBLIGATIONS

CREDITOR	BALANCE	PAYMENT	NO. LEFT	INT. RATE	WHAT PURCHASED	DUE DATE
				9.5		
TOTAL						

ORDER OF DEBT REPAYMENT

Which debt should you pay off first? People often begin with the one with the highest interest rate. However that may not be the best order of attack. A better plan is to use the form on the following page to list each debt you have by its outstanding balance and then divide each debt by its monthly payment (principal and interest).

I Corinthians 14:40

Everything should be done in a fitting and orderly way.

The one with the lowest balance-to-payment quotient is the one to focus on liquidating first.

Pay as much as you possibly can above the payment until that debt is paid in full. Once it is paid off, take the monthly payment plus the additional prepayment you were making and apply it as additional principal to the next one on the Order of Debt Repayment form on the following page. Once that debt is liquidated you will have even a larger amount to apply as a prepayment of principal on the next debt in the order of attack.

In most cases the house mortgage will be the one with the largest quotient and hence, the last one on which you will focus. However, by that time, all other debts will be paid off and you will have the total of all the previous payments to apply as prepaid principal on the house mortgage. Such a large prepayment of principal each month will dramatically decrease the remaining term of the mortgage.

ORDER OF DEBT REPAYMENT

DEBT BALANCE	MONTHLY PAYMENT	QUOTIENT (Column 1 ÷ Column 2)	ORDER OF ATTACK*
	TOTAL		

*enter #1 for the lowest quotient and
enter #2 for the next lowest, etc.

CHAPTER 5

THE "GRACE OF GIVING"

NOTICE:

It defies logic that 90% of your income can go farther than 100%. God's Word says it can. What you will read in this section is a practical guide for putting God first in your life and thereby involving heaven in your personal finances.

Recognizing the preferred status of the tithe, together with proper money management, will in time solve any money problem. Because of the profound effect these truths can have upon your financial destiny, purpose here and now to diligently apply them.

II Corinthians 8:7

...excel in this grace of giving.

Proverbs 3:4-6 (TLB)

If you want favor with both God and man, and a reputation for good judgment and common sense, then trust the Lord completely; don't ever trust yourself. In everything you do, put God first, and he will direct you and crown your efforts with success.

GOD TAKES TITHING SERIOUSLY

The word "tithe" means ten percent. But as used in the Scripture, it is always the first ten percent - the *first* and the *best*. It must never be the leftovers. IT BELONGS TO THE LORD and is to be treated as something you owe although it should not be viewed as just another bill to pay. It is holy.

Take care to always treat the tithe as HOLY. To the greatest extent practical, keep it separate from other funds and offer it to God as quickly as possible.

A tithe can never be more than ten percent. Any amount above the tithe is referred to in Scripture as an offering or a free-will gift.

God *demands* the tithe and he *deserves* the offerings.

Leviticus 27:30-33

A tithe of everything from the land, whether grain from the soil or fruit from the trees, belongs to the Lord; it is holy to the Lord. If a man redeems any of his tithe, he must add a fifth of the value to it. The entire tithe of the herd and flock—every tenth animal that passes under the shepherd's rod—will be holy to the Lord. He must not pick out the good from the bad or make substitution, both the animal and its substitute become holy and cannot be redeemed.

AVOID THE CURSE OF POVERTY AND CLAIM THE ABUNDANCE

- Can you afford not to pay tithes?
- Non-givers are under a curse.

  See **Achan's sin** (Joshua 7:17-21)—the whole nation suffered from one man's greed. Likewise, a church's overall effectiveness may be limited by the sin of only a few members.

  God had promised the children of Israel ten cities. Jericho was the first. In God's economy, the *first* tenth belonged to him and was to be consecrated at his altar.

- To take all or part of the Lord's portion brings a curse.

  The tithe you embezzle will be devoured by Satan. It will not improve your standard of living, help you acquire extra assets or get you out of debt sooner. It will be destroyed. You can't afford not to tithe because when the tithe is offered back to God in faith, it opens the "windows of heaven" and God imparts wisdom to make the remaining 90% accomplish far more than 100% would under the curse.

- There are still curses in this dispensation of grace.

Malachi 3:8,9

Will a man rob God? Yet you rob me. "But you ask, 'How do we rob you?' In tithes and offerings. You are under a curse—the whole nation of you—because you are robbing me."

Proverbs 11:24,25

One man gives freely, yet gains even more; another withholds unduly but comes to poverty. A generous man will prosper.

Joshua 6:18

But keep away from the devoted* (Hebrew, *cherem)* thing. So that you will not bring about your own destruction* (*cherem*) by taking any of them.

*These words (devoted and destruction) are translated "accursed" in the KJV. It is something dedicated for sacrifice to God. It must be destroyed with no personal gain.

See Revelation 22:18,19

The last chapter of Revelation speaks of a curse.

See Acts 5:1-11

Ananias and Sapphira

It is a serious matter to lie to the Holy Spirit.

It is a serious matter to steal from God.

Genesis 2:16-17

And the Lord God commanded the man, "You are free to eat from any tree in the garden; but you must not eat from the tree of the knowledge of good and evil."

THE ORIGIN OF TITHING

- Tithing dates back to the Garden of Eden where God reserved something for himself.

  Adam could eat of all the trees of the garden except one (a picture of tithing).

- The first murder was committed over tithing.

  Abel brought from the *firstborn* of his flock; Cain simply brought an offering.

  Many mistakenly believe that Abel's offering was accepted because it involved the shedding of blood.

  Abel's sacrifice complied with the principle of tithing and it was offered in faith.

Genesis 4:3-5

In the course of time Cain brought *some* of the fruits of the soil as an offering to the Lord. But Abel brought fat portions from some of the *firstborn* of his flock. The Lord looked with favor on Abel and his offering, but on Cain and his offering he did not look with favor. So Cain was very angry, and his face was downcast. Then the Lord said to Cain, "Why are you angry? Why is your face downcast? If you do what is right, will you not be accepted?"

Hebrews 11:4

By faith Abel offered God a better sacrifice than Cain did. By faith he was commended as a righteous man, when God spoke well of his offerings.

God accepted the firstfruits of non-animal offerings many times throughout Scripture.

KEY TRUTH

The tithe must be the *first* ten per cent of your income.

See also:

Exodus 22:29 Leviticus 2:12-16
Numbers 18:4,12 Nehemiah 10:35-39
Jeremiah 2:3 Romans 11:16

TITHING PREDATES THE MOSAIC LAW

It is a costly mistake to minimize the importance of the tithe. Some Christians mistakenly believe that the tithe is a legalism affecting only Old Testament Jews under the Mosaic law and has no significance for New Testament believers today.

- Two examples in Genesis of tithing before the Law

1. **Abram** offered the tithe to God through Melchizedec 425 years before the Law. (Genesis 14)

After rescuing his nephew, Lot, he was in route to return the plunder back to the king of Sodom. God sent Melchizedek to collect God's portion first.

The Lord had to send Melchizedec, a type

II Chronicles 31:5

As soon as the order went out, the Israelites generously gave the firstfruits of their grain, new wine, oil and honey and all that the fields produced...a tithe of everything.

Proverbs 3:9.10

Honor the Lord with your wealth, with the firstfruits of all your crops; *then* your barns will be filled to overflowing, and your vats will brim over with new wine.

of Christ (Hebrews 7), to prevent Abram from making a serious mistake that would have limited God's right to bless him.

Because of Abraham's obedience God blessed him.

2. After **Jacob's ladder dream** at Bethel, Jacob vowed two things to God (Genesis 28:20-22):

    1. The Lord will be my God.
    2. Of all you give me, I will give you a tenth.

TITHING CODIFIED INTO THE MOSAIC LAW

Later, this practice observed by Adam, Abel, Abraham and others pre-dating the Law was codified into the Law. (Leviticus 27:30)

Study the following examples of tithing:

- The restoration of the Lord's Tithe under Hezekiah (II Chronicles 31:2-5)
- Aaron's Tithe (Numbers 18:25-28)—a tithe of the Lord's Tithe
- The Rejoicing Tithe (Deuteronomy 14:22-29)—a tithe paid to oneself
- The Third Year Tithe (Deuteronomy 26:12-16)—a tithe for the welfare of the underprivileged.

Genesis 15:1

After this, the word of the Lord came to Abram in a vision: "Do not be afraid, Abram. I am your shield, and your reward will be very great."

Genesis 28:20-22

Then Jacob made a vow, saying, "If God will be with me and will watch over me on this journey I am taking and will give me food to eat and clothes to wear so that I return safely to my father's house, then the Lord will be my God and this stone that I have set up as a pillar will be God's house, and all that you give me I will give you a tenth."

THE TESTIMONY OF MALACHI

Less than 400 years before the birth of Jesus, the Hebrews had forsaken God's tithing principle. It was a period remarkably similar to ours.

(Notice that tithes is in the plural form. See the four tithes listed on the preceeding page.)

God authorizes you to validate the promises to the tither by testing the procedure.

Malachi called for three things:

1. Repentance

You must prayerfully seek God concerning how far back you should go in making restitution for unpaid tithes.

Many times a sacrificial offering given in contrition as a token of past remissions will clear the conscience toward God of the guilt of robbing him.

Malachi 3:7-12

"Return to me and I will return to you," says the Lord Almighty.

"But you ask, 'How are we to return?'

"Will a man rob God? Yet you rob me."

"But you ask, 'How do we rob you?'

"in tithes and offerings. You are under a curse—the whole nation of you—because you are robbing me. Bring the whole tithe into the storehouse, that there may be food in my house. Test me in this," says the Lord Almighty, "and see if I will not throw open the floodgates of heaven and pour out so much blessing that you will not have room enough for it. I will prevent pests from devouring your crops, and the vines in your fields will not cast their fruit," says the Lord Almighty. "Then all the nations will call you blessed, for yours will be a delightful land," says the Lord Almighty.

I John 1:9

If we confess our sins, he is faithful and just and will forgive us our sins and purify us from all unrighteousness.

2. Restoration of tithing

3. Giving to the storehouse

From the time of Hezekiah there was a storehouse for depositing tithes and offerings. The New Testament counterpart to the storehouse is the local church.

II Chronicles 31:11,12

Hezekiah gave orders to prepare storerooms in the temple of the Lord, and this was done. Then they faithfully brought in the contribution, tithes and dedicated gifts.

FOUR REWARDS OF TITHING FOUND IN MALACHI

1. There will be no lack of money to carry out the administration of the local church and for the completion of the Great Commission.

2. There will be an opening of the floodgates of heaven. (KJV—"windows of heaven")

   How widely the windows will open is based entirely upon your generosity. You establish the measure of the flow of blessings, success and prosperity from the floodgates.

3. There will be a rebuking of whatever devours, devalues or destroys, such as inflation, recession and deterioration.

4. There will be recognition from unbelievers of the Lord's blessing.

See also
Malachi 3:12
II Chronicles 32:23

See the study on Luke 6:38 found on page 77 of this chapter.

John 10:10

The thief comes only to *steal* and kill and destroy; I have come that they may have life and have it to the full.

TITHING WAS APPROVED BY THE LORD JESUS

- Jesus did not come to do away with the Law

  He came to satisfy its demands.
  He came to fulfill it.
  He came to clarify it.
  He came to simplify it.

- Some aspects of the Law are relinquished for a higher authority.

  For example, it is no longer required that a blood sacrifice be made because Jesus' blood was given as the ultimate sacrifice.

- Tithing has never been abrogated or abolished.

- Tithing equates to making a sacrifice.

  For the past 2,000 years, the rendering of tithes and offerings to the Lord is the closest thing to sacrificing. When you offer money to the Lord, you give yourself to him. Since you have exchanged a part of your life for the money, the money you offer to God represents your life.

Matthew 5:17

Do not think that I have come to abolish the Law or the Prophets; I have not come to abolish them but to *fulfill* them.

II Timothy 3:16

All Scripture is God-breathed and is useful for teaching, rebuking, correcting and training in righteousness, so that the man of God may be thoroughly equipped for every good work.

Matthew 23:23

Woe to you, teachers of the law and Pharisees, you hypocrites! You give a tenth of your spices—mint, dill and cummin, but you have neglected the more important matters of the law—justice, mercy and faithfulness. *You should have practiced the latter without neglecting the former.*

TITHING WAS A PART OF THE APOSTLES' TEACHING

The apostles, prophets, evangelists, pastors, teachers and needy saints were supported by tithes and freewill offerings.

I Corinthians 16:2

On the first day of every week, each one of you should set aside a sum of money in keeping with his income.

Deuteronomy 14:22,23

Be sure to set aside a tenth...so that you may learn to revere the Lord your God always.

THE PURPOSES FOR TITHES AND OFFERINGS

1. **To learn to always fear (revere or honor) the Lord.** (See Malachi 1:6-8)

I Chronicles 29:14

Everything comes from you, and we have given you only what comes from your hand.

2. **To establish a weekly reminder of God's ownership.**

   Tithing is an external evidence of an internal commitment.

   Tithing is an outward expression of an inward attitude.

II Chronicles 31:4-5

He ordered the people living in Jerusalem to give the portion due the priest and Levities so they could devote themselves to the Law of the Lord. As soon as the order went out, the Israelites generously gave the firstfruits of their grain, new wine, oil and honey and all that the fields produced. They brought a great amount, a tithe of everything.

3. **To support the ministry and outreach of your local church.**

The Levites (tribe of priests) received no apportionment of land but their inheritance was the tithe to support the ministry to the Lord.

Numbers 18:21-24

I give to the Levites all the tithes in Israel as their inheritance in return for the work they do while serving at the Tent of Meeting...They will receive no inheritance among the Israelites. Instead, I give to the Levities as their inheritance the tithes that the Israelites present as an offering to the Lord.

The Lord *commands* that a minister be remunerated from the people to whom he ministers.

I Corinthians 9:7-14

Who serves as a soldier at his own expense? Who plants a vineyard and does not eat of its grapes?...Doesn't the Law say the same thing? For it is written in the Law of Moses: "Do not muzzle an ox while it is treading out the grain." Is it about oxen that God is concerned? Surely he says this for us, doesn't he? Yes, this was written for us, because when the plowman plows and the thresher threshes, they ought to do so in hope of sharing in the harvest. If we have sown spiritual seed among you, is it too much if we reap a material harvest from you?...Don't you know that those who work in the temple get their food from the temple, and those who serve at the altar share in what is offered on the altar. In the same way, the Lord has <u>commanded</u> that those who preach the gospel should receive their living from the gospel.

Galatians 6:6

Anyone who receives instruction in the Word *must* share all good things with his instructor.

Preachers and teachers are to receive double "honorarium." The Greek for "honor" (*time*) means pecuniary remuneration for services. It is elsewhere translated as "pay" or "price." (Matthew 27:6,9; Acts 4:34; 7:16; I Corinthians 6:20)

I Timothy 5:17,18

The elders who direct the affairs of the church well are worthy of *double honor,* especially those whose work is preaching and teaching. (Williams Translation: "...considered as deserving twice the salary they get.")

Jesus would not minister where the people refused to give.

John 4:44

Now Jesus himself had pointed out that a prophet has no honor (Gk. *time*) in his own country.

A minister's *total* expenses should be underwritten.

Matthew 10:10

Take no bag for the journey, or extra tunic or sandals or a staff; for the worker is worthy of his keep.

4. Because it is good for you.

God does not need your money. You need to give.

Being faithful in tithing will do far more for you than the mere money you give will do for the Kingdom.

Acts 20:35

The Lord Jesus himself said: "It is more blessed to give than to receive."

> **KEY TRUTH**
> **The tithe, offered joyfully in expectant faith, frees God to control what he owns anyway— the remaining 90% —and multiply it.**

SEVEN WAYS TITHES AND OFFERINGS MUST BE OFFERED IN ORDER TO OBTAIN MAXIMUM RESULTS

1. First give yourself to God.

II Corinthians 8:3-5

They gave as much as they were able and even beyond their ability…but they gave themselves first to the Lord.

2. Cheerfully

- The Greek for "cheerful" is *hilaros* from which we get the English word hilarious.

II Corinthians 9:7

God loves a cheerful giver.

3. Not grudgingly

II Corinthians 9:5

Not as one grudgingly given...

4. With contemplation

II Corinthians 9:5

...Each man should give what he has decided in his heart to give...

5. Without reluctance

II Corinthians 9:5

Give...not reluctantly...

6. Without pressure

II Corinthians 9:5

Give...not under compulsion.

7. In faith, expecting a harvest

Hebrews 11:4

By faith Abel offered God a better sacrifice than Cain did.

Galatians 6:7

A man reaps what he sows.

- What you give is what you receive.
- How much you receive is determined by the measure you use.

Luke 6:38

Give and it will be given to you. A good measure, pressed down, shaken together and running over, will be poured into your lap. For with the measure you use, it will be measured to you.

- Expect both temporal and eternal rewards.

Mark 10:29,30

"I tell you the truth," Jesus replied, "No one who has left home or brothers or sisters or mother or father or children or fields for me and the gospel will fail to receive a hundred times as much in this present age (homes, brothers, sisters, mothers, children and fields—and with them, persecutions) and in the age to come, eternal life."

- Temporal rewards often come with persecutions from:

  Satan
  Friends
  "Pharisees"

- Paul did not separate giving from receiving.

Philippians 4:15-20

Moreover, as you Philippians know, in the early day of your acquaintance with the gospel, when I set out from Macedonia, not one church shared with me in the matter of giving and receiving, except you only; for even when I was in Thessalonica, you sent me aid again and again when I was in need. Not that I am looking for a gift, but I am looking for what may be credited to your account. I have received full payment and even more; I am amply supplied now that I have received from Epaphroditus the gifts you sent. They are a fragrant offering, an acceptable sacrifice pleasing to God. And my God will meet all your needs according to His glorious riches in Christ Jesus.

- Paul was eager for a gift even though his needs were amply supplied.
- Giving credits to the heavenly account.
- If the gift is acceptable to God, he promises to meet all needs through Jesus and his anointing.

- Consider the time factor between sowing and harvesting.

Galatians 6:9

Let us not become weary in doing good, for at the proper time we will reap a harvest *if* we do not give up.

Hebrews 6:12

We do not want you to become lazy, but to imitate those who through faith and patience inherit what has been promised.

- Persevere through faith and patience.

Luke 16:10

Whoever can be trusted with very little can also be trusted with much, and whoever is dishonest with very little will also be dishonest with much.

When God can trust his people with money, he sees to it that they always have plenty for themselves and others.

II Corinthians 9:6,10,11

Remember this: Whoever sows sparingly will also reap sparingly and whoever sows generously will also reap generously. Now he who supplies seed to the sower and bread for food will also supply and increase your store of seed and will enlarge the harvest of your righteousness. You will be made rich in every way *so that* you can be generous on every occasion and through us your generosity will result in thanksgiving to God.

If you can't give to God in your present situation, you probably won't give to him when you have abundance either.

HOW SHOULD YOU GIVE?

1. Out of obedience

   You are commanded to give without selfish aim or profit motive.

Romans 11:35

Who has ever given to God that God should repay him?

2. Out of abundance

   You are to give from your increase.

I Corinthians 16:2 (KJV)

Upon the first day of the week let everyone of you lay by him in store, *as God hath prospered him.*

Hebrews 13:16

And do not forget to do good and to share with others, for with such sacrifices God is pleased.

3. Sacrificially, yielding your wants and needs for others

   Sacrificial giving is almost unknown in this country.

   Perhaps it could be sacrificing the country club, or bowling or foregoing the purchase of a new car or the building of a swimming pool or giving of your time.

II Corinthians 8:2-4,12

Out of the most severe trial, their overflowing joy and their extreme poverty welled up in rich generosity. For I testify that they gave as much as they were able and even beyond their ability...they urgently pleaded with us for the privilege of sharing in the service to the saints. For if the willingness is there, the gift is acceptable according to what one has.

- The amount is not as important as the attitude.

Mark 12:41-43

Jesus sat down opposite the place where the offerings were put and watched the crowd putting their money into the temple treasury. Many rich people threw in large amounts. But a poor widow came and put in two very small copper coins, worth only a fraction of a penny. Calling his disciples to him, Jesus said, "I tell you the truth, this poor widow has put more into the treasury than all the others. They all gave out of their wealth; but she, out of her poverty (KJV—"out of her want"), put in everything—all she had to live on."

4. As a memorial to God

Psalm 50:14,15

Sacrifice thank offerings to God, fulfill your vows to the Most High, and call upon me in the day of trouble; I will deliver you, and you will honor me.

Study the following examples of those whose gifts were a memorial to God:

- The **Widow at Zarephath** (I Kings 17:7-16)

  The meal was running out until she added giving to her prayer.

- **Hannah** "bargains" with God (I Samuel 1)
- **Poor widow at the treasury** (see reference on previous page)
- **Cornelius**

Acts 10:1-4,30,31

He and all his family were devout and God-fearing; he gave generously to those in need and prayed to God regularly....Suddenly a man in shining clothes stood before me and said, "Cornelius, God has heard your prayers and remembered your gifts to the poor..."

- The **woman breaking the alabaster box** (Mark 14:3-9)

GOD PRONOUNCES A SPECIAL BLESSING ON THOSE WHO CARE FOR THE NEEDY

1. Make God your debtor.

Proverbs 19:17

He who is kind to the poor lends to the Lord, and *he will reward him for what he has done.*

2. There are special instructions that, when followed, will result in reward.

Matthew 6:3,4

But *when* you give to the needy, do not let your left hand know what your right hand is doing, so that your giving may be in secret. Then your Father, who sees what is done in secret, *will reward you.*

3. Even the minutest giving will be rewarded.

Matthew 10:42

And if anyone gives a cup of cold water to one of these little ones because he is my disciple, I tell you the truth, *he will certainly not lose his reward.*

4. The Law of Gleaning

Deuteronomy 24:19-21

When you are harvesting in your field and you overlook a sheaf, do not go back to get it. Leave it for the alien, the fatherless and the widow, *so that the Lord your God may bless you in all the work of your hands.*

5. Jesus taught giving to the needy.

See Matthew 6:3,4 above. Jesus uses the word "when" not "if."

I John 3:16,17

This is how we know what love is: Jesus Christ laid down his life for us. And we ought to lay down our lives for our brothers. If anyone has material possessions and sees his brother in need but has no pity on him, how can the love of God be in him?

6. The Early Church practiced giving to the needy.

See the example of the Macedonia Church (I Corinthians 16)

CHAPTER 6

BUDGETING

Budgeting is a plan for the wise coordination of what God has entrusted to your supervision. A budget is needed to rectify past financial mistakes, and a budget is necessary to keep you on track once financial equilibrium is attained.

The major justification for a budget is to preserve the sanctity of the seed—that is *to insure that after all costs of living have been met, there is money left over to be used as seed.*

SIGNALS THAT YOU NEED A BUDGET

- ☐ Finding it difficult to pay the Lord's tithe
- ☐ Letting one or more bills slide into next month
- ☐ Finding it difficult to maintain an adequate checking account balance
- ☐ Frequently having to juggle money between savings and checking accounts
- ☐ Finding it impossible to save money
- ☐ Finding yourself in a cash crunch just before payday
- ☐ Frequently asking yourself, "Where did all my money go?"

WHAT IS A BUDGET?

- Planned or controlled spending
- A means to make your money go farther
- A series of rules and boundaries

Proverbs 24:3,4 (TLB)

Any enterprise is built by wise planning, becomes strong through common sense and profits wonderfully by keeping abreast of the facts.

Proverbs 22:3 (TLB)

A prudent man foresees the difficulties ahead and prepares for them; the simpleton goes blindly on and suffers the consequences.

- A way of telling your money where to go—not trying to figure out where it went
- A plan, a roadmap
- A tool to help you establish priorities
- A forecast of how your money is to be spent

Proverbs 14:16 (TLB)

A wise man is cautious and avoids danger; a fool plunges ahead with great confidence.

WITHOUT A BUDGET...

1. You will tend to spend more than you make.

    Most families will earn in excess of $1 million in a lifetime.

    Most families will spend in excess of $1 million in a lifetime.

2. You will be undisciplined, buying what you want until the money runs out. Unfortunately, the yearning exceeds the earning.
3. You will be unaware of where your money goes.
4. You will have financial chaos and family tension.

If you haven't already, you will soon be entering the computer age and investing in a personal computer. You will find a vast array of bookkeeping software programs available to you.

A top-selling personal financial software package is Quicken published by Intuit, with a suggested retail price of around $39. The Quicken screen looks just like your paper checkbook, prints checks, updates your register, categorizes your spending, reconciles your bank account, slashes data entry time (type a few characters and it instantly fills in the rest), provides reports and graphs, produces profit and loss statements and balance sheets, forecasts cash flow and

more. It has a wonderful budgeting section and another section will organize and keep track of your investments. Quicken is a single entry bookkeeping system.

For those of you who operate a small business or prefer a double entry system, consider QuickBooks also by Intuit. QuickBooks does everything Quicken does plus much, much more. It has a general ledger, journals, accounts payable, accounts receivable, invoicing, inventory, etc. It can be purchased for around $100.

STEPS IN BUILDING A WORKABLE BUDGET

A budget is not just a record of past expenses but a *forecast* of future expenses. Preparation of a meaningful budget will depend largely on the first step—obtaining accurate records of past spending.

1. Take a serious look at your financial goals.

Your primary goal should be to live *below* your means so you will be able to pay tithes, liquidate debt, build an emergency fund, consistently invest money each month, give generously and thereby live a life free of financial pressures and worries.

Write down your financial goals and objectives.

"See" them accomplished with the eyes of faith. By faith, visualize exactly what you and your family will look and be like once these financial objectives are finally realized.

Set short-range goals and keep them realistic.

Establishing a few realistic goals and finding that with God's help you can achieve them, will give you a sense of satisfaction and the confidence you need to tackle the long-range goals.

Habakkuk 2:2 (KJV)

"Write the vision, and make it plain...that he may run that readeth it."

Set long-range goals.

Of course, not everyone in the family is going to agree on everything, so, at the start, focus on long-range goals that may take years to achieve, such as funds for retirement, education for the children, buying a new house, etc. Sacrifice is easier if you have a reason. Example: Jacob working for Rachel (Genesis 29:20)

Set mid-range goals.

Next, set those goals you hope to reach within six months to five years. To avoid all-out war in the family, list your mid-range goals in order of importance and give them reasonable price tags. This will help establish your priorities.

Create a detailed plan of action.

Create a detailed plan of action to get you to the desired destination. Remember the message in the Book of James: "Faith without accompanying actions is useless." (See James 2:17)

In summary

Goals must be in writing, have specific steps of action to accomplish them, must have a time frame and must have a price tag.

2. Become familiar with the "Money and the Christian" forms.

See the pages, beginning on page 93 of this book, entitled "Instructions for Using *Money and the Christian* Forms", for step-by-step instructions detailing where to get the information you need and what to do with it once it is accumulated. Be sure to read the instructions for each form as it is referred to in this chapter.

3. Review your spending history and fill out the SPENDING REPORT form to start the budget.

Analyze and record your expenses and income for the past six months. The purpose is to help you determine how you have spent your money for the past six months. (See page 95, "Two purposes for the SPENDING REPORT form" for instructions on initially setting up the budget.)

4. *Fill out the Budget Worksheet form.*

See page 95 for help.

5. *Fill out the Budget Payment Per Pay Period form if needed.*

Use this form *only* if you are paid more than once a month and need to stagger the payment of your bills to coincide with your pay periods.

6. *Determine your resources.*

Fill out the Income Statement form and figure your monthly take-home pay and other sources of income such as interest, etc. See page 95 for help.

7. *Now continue the budget from this month forward.*

See page 93.

There are two budgets you will be dealing with—the *interim* and the *ideal.* The interim is the temporary budget you will use until you can achieve the ideal. The interim allows you to put more money into the areas that needs attention now—such as paying off a debt.

By following the seven steps above you should have a better idea what you are spending and how much your actual income is.

TIPS TO CONSIDER WHEN CREATING YOUR BUDGET

- ***Eliminate consumer debt.***

  If you have accumulated a sizeable consumer debt and are now paying only the minimum payments required, face the facts. The bulk of your payments is interest. By continuing to pay only the minimum, it will take you many years to attain the desired debt-free status. Your first goal should be to eliminate this consumer debt as soon as possible. Follow the strategies taught in Chapter 4 to accelerate the debt reduction process.

- ***Agree as a family on how much you will apply to debt reduction each month.***

  Set aside a *fixed* amount of money each month for debt reduction—as much as you can possibly afford even if you have to use your savings. Usually the interest *charged* on consumer debt is considerably more than interest *earned* on savings. Why pay high interest on credit card debt while earning low interest on savings? Don't count on monies left over to apply toward debt reduction.

- ***Establish an emergency fund.***

  It is a good idea to have a reserve fund to use in the event of an unexpected major expense. Ideally a family should have an emergency fund of five to six months of take-home pay set aside to cover all but the most staggering setbacks. Once you have an emergency fund, you can safely save for your goals and begin a long-range investment program. If you're starting the fund at zero, you should budget a monthly amount for your emergency fund the same way you will budget for any other expense.

Proverbs 6:6-8 (TLB)

Take a lesson from the ants, you lazy fellow. Learn from their ways and be wise...they labor hard all summer, gathering food for the winter.

- ***Build savings for future expenses into the budget.***

Instead of savings being "what's left over, if anything," it should be a predetermined amount. Fund savings as regularly and faithfully as you pay the Lord's tithe or your mortgage payment.

Look into the future, determine what you will need to spend, and start preparing now. For example: you know your car insurance premium of $600 will be due in six months. Divide the amount needed, ($600), by 6 (six months), and start setting aside $100 a month so when your insurance bill comes due, there will be sufficient money to cover it. Use this procedure with each of the major upcoming bills in your life. Once the amount needed is accumulated for the item, you can buy it without guilt.

If you have trouble disciplining yourself to set aside monies, have your company do it for you, in their payroll savings plan. One budget management expert suggested leaving your savings in a bank account on the other side of town, so, "When you're tempted to make a withdrawal, you'll find you're too lazy to bother."

Luke 14:28

Suppose one of you wants to build a tower. Will he not first sit down and estimate the cost to see if he has enough money to complete it?

- ***Keep records of all cash expenditures.***

Don't panic! This is a 30-day exercise to determine what you are actually spending. Budget experts say that, ideally, you should carry a notebook and keep track of all cash expenditures, even cokes and/or candy out of vending machines, for at least a month, to establish a spending history. Then you can *make decisions based on knowledge* of what you are truly spending.

- ***Stay on course.***

  You, or someone in the family, will need to keep books to see that the budget stays on target. The bookkeeping does not need to be complicated. It will help to pay for all items over $10 with checks and let the check register serve as your expense record. Once a month, you can pull out all your checks and credit card statements, and tally these expenses onto the SPENDING REPORT form.

- ***Get organized.***

  Keep it simple—keep all your records in one place! For example, buy a box of manila file folders and label twelve of them, January through December. Keep all your cancelled checks, cash receipts, credit card vouchers and statements in the file folder for the appropriate month. At the end of the year all your records are in file folders and most importantly, are all in one place.

- ***Annual budgetary checkup.***

  As time passes, some fine-tuning will be needed because invariably there will be expenses you hadn't considered. Once you've modified your spending behavior, an annual checkup is enough, unless you are faced with a major financial change.

- ***Don't be too hard on yourself.***

  One word of warning: Don't get carried away. Putting a budget to work and living on an austerity program can seriously strain any relationship. Everyone needs some luxuries from time to time. "Each member in the family should be allowed to keep one indulgence," says one financial planner. Don't become so detail conscious that the budget controls your whole life.

INSTRUCTIONS FOR USING MONEY AND THE CHRISTIAN FORMS

FILLING OUT THE "SPENDING REPORT" FORM (PAGE 98)

(Don't write on any of the blank forms until you make copies of them.)

There are two sets of forms. One set shows examples and has page numbers. The second set is blank and is for you to copy for your own use.

- Each month should have its own SPENDING REPORT forms.

  Make copies of the forms and use as many sheets for the month as you need.

  Column 1 is for your check number.
  Columns 2 and 3 are self-explanatory.
  Column 4 is for the total amount on the check.
  Columns 5-16 are for expense categories.
  Column 17 is a space to write any single expense heading.
  Column 18 is for the dollar amount of the expense shown in Column 17.

- As you can see there are not columns for every expense account. The purpose of the columns is for ease of totaling when you have many checks for one expense category.

  You can use the "Miscellaneous Description" column for single items which do not require a full column.

- One check may be divided into any number of expense categories. For example, your check to the grocery store may include food and antifreeze for your car, so food will be shown in Column 7 and antifreeze will be shown on the same line but in Column 9.

- Deposit your total pay check into the bank.

- To get spending cash, make yourself a check payable to "Cash." Keep the receipts of how the cash is spent. At the end of the month, record the amount of the receipts into the appropriate expense columns.

How to record the check to savings for future purchases

- Each month make out a check to your savings account. The amount of this check will have been determined while you were figuring the budget. Perhaps you are putting aside \$175 a month—\$20 toward children's clothing, \$100 toward car insurance, \$25 toward car repair and \$30 toward vacation. Your SPENDING REPORT form will show \$175 in Column 4 with each of the items broken down into the proper expense columns across the row.

  At the end of each month, when the columns are totaled, the check(s) made out to savings will be totaled and put on line 32 under the proper category heading. These totals will be "posted" to the individual SAVINGS SUMMARY forms.

How to record credit card purchases

- The payments on your cards are also recorded here. Remember, nothing is to be charged if it cannot be paid off within the 25-day grace period. So, when you pay your credit card statement, divide the expenses into the proper columns.

- If you are paying off an old balance, include what you are paying in the Extra Debt Reduction category, but be sure the interest portion is put under Interest Expense. Interest is not part of your debt reduction. When you are filling out the BUDGET WORKSHEET form, the Extra Debt Reduction is included in the MISCELLANEOUS TOTAL.

Reconciling your SPENDING REPORT form

- When you total Column 4 at the end of the month, it must agree with the checks written from your checkbook.

- Make sure your figures are balancing by adding Columns 5 through 18 across. The total must equal the amount in Column 4.

- Line 33 is Line 31 minus the amount on Line 32.

- In order to summarize and see clearly how much you have spent, and where it was

spent, it is necessary to "post" the monthly totals to a summary sheet. (See "Filling out the SPENDING SUMMARY form on page 96.)

Two purposes for the SPENDING REPORT form

1. To categorize the data for creating the budget the first time.

    (This is a onetime action.) List all your checks and credit card statements from the past six months. Be sure and pick up all routine monthly costs, including lump sums such as insurance, school tuition, gifts, etc. It is not necessary to keep each month separate when reconstructing this data.

    Total each column for all six months and divide by 6 (months). This gives you a rough average per month to be used to create the BUDGET WORKSHEET form.

2. As a check register for future spending.

    The above instructions apply for both.

FILLING OUT THE "INCOME STATEMENT" FORM (PAGE 100)

- This form allows you to record your monthly take-home pay. Don't forget to record interest or dividends earned on your investments and/or savings accounts.
- Deposit your full paycheck into the bank. Withdraw your spending money by making a check to cash.

FILLING OUT THE "BUDGET WORKSHEET" FORM (PAGE 102)

- The capitalized, reverse-type lines are the expense categories. These are the same as on the SPENDING REPORT forms. You will be working with the six month's average for each expense category you have previously calculated from the SPENDING REPORT form. Fill in the BUDGET

WORKSHEET form using those figures. You can go into as much detail as you wish. You can fill in only the totals on the reverse-type total line or you can show the detail that comprises that total.

- Refer to the suggestions given earlier concerning tips on setting up your budget.
- Indicate with an asterisk (*) any amounts to be put into savings for future expenses such as an annual insurance premium. When you have completed this form, total all figures with the asterisk (*) and place that amount in the Savings Total at the bottom of Column 2.
- Now, here's where prayer and determination come into play. *The total figure on this page cannot exceed the figure on the bottom line of your "Income Statement" form.* In other words the TOTAL CATEGORIES line has to be less than your take-home pay. There has to be some seed left over to plant. Rework the figures on the BUDGET WORKSHEET form until it is less. Don't despair. It may take seven or eight attempts, but it will be worth it in the end. In the beginning the Total Categories line may be only a few dollars less than your take-home pay but eventually it should be a *minimum* of ten percent less, ideally even more.

FILLING OUT THE "SPENDING SUMMARY" FORM (PAGE 104)

- You will create individual sheets for each expense category you are using. At the end of each month "post" the month's total from the SPENDING REPORT form to these individual sheets. In other words, you will have a sheet for each of the expense categories on the BUDGET WORKSHEET form.
- Each sheet will show, monthly, and year-to-date, how much you are spending in that expense category.

FILLING OUT THE "SAVING SUMMARY" FORM (PAGE 105)

- The SAVINGS SUMMARY form is similar to the SPENDING SUMMARY form. They are individual sheets, with headings of the various expense categories you are accumulating savings toward—vacation, auto, etc. You will be posting the totals from Line 32 of the SPENDING REPORT form to the proper expense categories in the column entitled Deposited.
- The SAVINGS SUMMARY form has one difference from the SPENDING SUMMARY form—the money will be removed when it is spent. The SAVINGS SUMMARY sheets are an accounting of monies

that will be spent in the future. By totaling the balances on all the sheets, you can determine exactly how much you have in your savings plan. At any point, you will know exactly how much you have accumulated toward your insurance payment or toward your vacation, etc.

- For example, when it is time to pay your insurance premium, you will do four things:

  1. Make a withdrawal from your savings account for the amount needed to pay the premium. Put it into your checking account.

  2. Remove the amount from the Savings Summary sheet for the proper category (in this example, Insurance) by posting the amount under the column entitled Spent.

  3. Record the amount on the Income Statement form under From Savings.

  4. Write a check to your insurance company and record it on the Spending Report form, as you would any other check.

Think of the freedom you will experience, knowing you will not have the frustration and worry about where the money is coming from to pay a bill such as the insurance premium, or how you are going to finance the vacation. When you do spend the accumulated money, you can do so without guilt that the money should have been spent elsewhere.

Money and the CHRISTIAN

SPENDING REPORT

	(1) Check No.	(2) Date	(3) Description	(4) Amount of Check	(5) Contributions	(6) Clothing	(7) Food	(8) Housing	
1	101	1-1	Church	75.00	75.00				1
2	102	1-1	Sunbelt Mortgage	500.00				500.00	2
3	103	1-14	Walmart Superstore	124.60			117.09		3
4	104	1-16	Cash	50.00	10.00	12.60			4
5	105	1-20	Savings	175.00		20.00			5
6									6
7									7
8									8
9									9
10									10
11									11
12									12
13									13
14									14
15									15
16									16
17									17
18									18
19									19
20									20
21									21
22									22
23									23
24									24
25									25
26									26
27									27
28									28
29									29
30									30
31	SUBTOTAL:			924.60	85.00	32.60	117.09	500.00	31
32	LESS: Amount to Savings (Post to SAVING SUMMARY forms)					20.00			32
33	TOTAL: Post to SPENDING SUMMARY forms			924.60	85.00	12.60	117.09	500.00	33

Month of January

	(9) Auto Expense	(10)	(11)	(12)	(13)	(14)	(15)	(16)	(17) Misc. Description	(18) Amount
1										
2										
3	7.51									
4	27.40								car insur.	100.00
5	25.00								vacation	30.00
6										
7										
8										
9										
10										
11										
12										
13										
14										
15										
16										
17										
18										
19										
20										
21										
22										
23										
24										
25										
26										
27										
28										
29										
30										
31	59.91									130.00
32	25.00									130.00
33	34.91									-0-

INCOME STATEMENT

	(1) Date	(2) Description	(3) January	(4) February	(5) March	(6) April	(7) May	
1		Salary						1
2		Less: Withholding						2
3		Less: Social Security						3
4		Less: Insurance						4
5		Less: Other						5
6								6
7								7
8								8
9								9
10		Interest Income						10
11								11
12								12
13								13
14								14
15								15
16		Misc. Income						16
17								17
18								18
19								19
20								20
21		FROM SAVINGS						21
22								22
23								23
24								24
25								25
26								26
27								27
28								28
29								29
30								30
31								31
32								32
33	TOTAL:							33

INCOME STATEMENT (Continued)

	(8) June	(9) July	(10) August	(11) September	(12) October	(13) November	(14) December	(15) Year-To-Date	
1									1
2									2
3									3
4									4
5									5
6									6
7									7
8									8
9									9
10									10
11									11
12									12
13									13
14									14
15									15
16									16
17									17
18									18
19									19
20									20
21									21
22									22
23									23
24									24
25									25
26									26
27									27
28									28
29									29
30									30
31									31
32									32
33									33

BUDGET WORKSHEET

New clothing	______
Cleaning & repairs	______
New shoes & repairs	______
Patterns & notions for sewing	______
Cosmetics	______
CLOTHING/CLEANING TOTAL	$

Haircuts & personal care	______
Unbudgeted items that don't fit elsewhere	______
CONTINGENCY/ALLOWANCES TOTAL	$

Books, magazines, newspapers	______
College expense	______
Concert, lectures, music lessons	______
School supplies	______
EDUCATION TOTAL	$

Food eaten at home	______
Meals out	______
FOOD TOTAL	$

Church donations	______
Civic donations	______
Other	______
TITHES/CONTRIBUTIONS TOTAL	$

Mortgage	______
House Rent	______
Operating Expenses:	
House cleaning supplies	______
Electricity/light bulbs	______
Gas	______
Water	______
Labor costs/maid, etc.	______
Lawn care	______
Paper products	______
Stationery/stamps	______
Bank charges	______
Telephone	______
Tools and their repair	______
Repairs:	
Bathroom	______
Cleaning rugs, etc.	______
Electrical repairs	______
Plumbing repairs	______
Kitchen improvements	______
Landscaping	______
Bedrooms, paint, etc.	______
Furniture:	
Furniture	______
Blankets, sheets, etc	______
Drapes, rugs & linoleum	______
Dishes, glasses, silverware	______
Appliances bought or repaired	______
Garden equipment	______
HOUSING TOTAL	$

House & furniture	______
Health	______
Life	______
INSURANCE TOTAL	$

Doctor	______
Dentist	______
Eyeglasses	______
Medicines	______
Vitamins	______
MEDICAL TOTAL	$

Payments on loans	______
Extra debt reduction	______
Other	______
MISCELLANEOUS TOTAL	$

Baby sitting	______
Cameras and film	______
Entertainment	______
Hobbies & games	______
Pets and their upkeep	______
TV purchase & repair	______
Sporting equipment	______
Toys, play equipment	______
Vacations	______
RECREATION/VACATION TOTAL	$

Income tax deposits	______
Property taxes	______
TAXES/LICENSES/FEES TOTAL	$

Christmas cards, gifts, decorations	______
Flowers as gifts, funerals	______
Gifts to friends	______
GIFTS/CHRISTMAS TOTAL	$

Airline fares	______
Bus and taxi fares	______
Car payments	______
Car repair & licenses	______
Gasoline & oil	______
Car insurance	______
TRANSPORTATION TOTAL	$

*** SAVINGS TOTAL**	$

**** TOTAL CATEGORIES**	$

* Place an asterisk (*) by the amount under the category you wish to put in savings each month. Total these amounts and put the total in the SAVINGS TOTAL category.

** The total on this line has to be less than your take-home pay.

BUDGET PAYMENT PER PAY PERIOD

ACCOUNT NAME	PERIOD 1		PERIOD 2		PERIOD 3		PERIOD 4	
Clothing / Cleaning								
Contingency / Allowances								
Education								
Food								
Gifts / Christmas								
Housing								
Insurance								
Medical								
Miscellaneous								
Recreation / Vacation								
Taxes / Licenses / Fees								
Tithes / Contributions								
Transportation								
TO SAVINGS:								
Car Insurance								
Car Repairs								
Clothes								
Contingencies								
Education								
Miscellaneous Savings								
Recreation								
Repairs / Improvements								
Total Expenses								
Net Income Available								
Over / Under (Short)								

SPENDING SUMMARY FORM

ACCOUNT NAME:____________________ AMOUNT BUDGETED: $__________

DATE	NAME	SPENT		BALANCE	

SAVING SUMMARY FORM

ACCOUNT NAME:______________________ AMOUNT BUDGETED: $______________

DATE	NAME	DEPOSITED		SPENT		BALANCE	

The blank forms on the following pages are for you to copy and use.

SPENDING SUMMARY FORM

ACCOUNT NAME:____________________________ AMOUNT BUDGETED: $________________

DATE	NAME	SPENT		BALANCE	

SPENDING REPORT

	(1) Check No.	(2) Date	(3) Description	(4) Amount of Check	(5) Contributions	(6) Clothing	(7) Food	(8) Housing	
1									1
2									2
3									3
4									4
5									5
6									6
7									7
8									8
9									9
10									10
11									11
12									12
13									13
14									14
15									15
16									16
17									17
18									18
19									19
20									20
21									21
22									22
23									23
24									24
25									25
26									26
27									27
28									28
29									29
30									30
31	SUBTOTAL:								31
32	LESS: Amount to Savings (Post to SAVING SUMMARY forms)								32
33	TOTAL: Post to SPENDING SUMMARY forms								33

Month of ____________________

	(9) Auto Expense	(10)	(11)	(12)	(13)	(14)	(15)	(16)	(17) Misc. Description	(18) Amount	
1											1
2											2
3											3
4											4
5											5
6											6
7											7
8											8
9											9
10											10
11											11
12											12
13											13
14											14
15											15
16											16
17											17
18											18
19											19
20											20
21											21
22											22
23											23
24											24
25											25
26											26
27											27
28											28
29											29
30											30
31											31
32											32
33											33

INCOME STATEMENT

	(1) Date	(2) Description	(3) January	(4) February	(5) March	(6) April	(7) May	
1		Salary						1
2		Less: Withholding						2
3		Less: Social Security						3
4		Less: Insurance						4
5		Less: Other						5
6								6
7								7
8								8
9								9
10		Interest Income						10
11								11
12								12
13								13
14								14
15								15
16		Misc. Income						16
17								17
18								18
19								19
20								20
21		FROM SAVINGS						21
22								22
23								23
24								24
25								25
26								26
27								27
28								28
29								29
30								30
31								31
32								32
33	TOTAL:							33

Money and the CHRISTIAN

INCOME STATEMENT (Continued)

	(8) June	(9) July	(10) August	(11) September	(12) October	(13) November	(14) December	(15) Year-To-Date	
1									1
2									2
3									3
4									4
5									5
6									6
7									7
8									8
9									9
10									10
11									11
12									12
13									13
14									14
15									15
16									16
17									17
18									18
19									19
20									20
21									21
22									22
23									23
24									24
25									25
26									26
27									27
28									28
29									29
30									30
31									31
32									32
33									33

BUDGET WORKSHEET

New clothing	
Cleaning & repairs	
New shoes & repairs	
Patterns & notions for sewing	
Cosmetics	
CLOTHING/CLEANING TOTAL	$

Haircuts & personal care	
Unbudgeted items that don't fit elsewhere	
CONTINGENCY/ALLOWANCES TOTAL	$

Books, magazines, newspapers	
College expense	
Concert, lectures, music lessons	
School supplies	
EDUCATION TOTAL	$

Food eaten at home	
Meals out	
FOOD TOTAL	$

Church donations	
Civic donations	
Other	
TITHES/CONTRIBUTIONS TOTAL	$

Mortgage	
House Rent	
Operating Expenses:	
House cleaning supplies	
Electricity/light bulbs	
Gas	
Water	
Labor costs/maid, etc.	
Lawn care	
Paper products	
Stationery/stamps	
Bank charges	
Telephone	
Tools and their repair	
Repairs:	
Bathroom	
Cleaning rugs, etc.	
Electrical repairs	
Plumbing repairs	
Kitchen improvements	
Landscaping	
Bedrooms, paint, etc.	
Furniture:	
Furniture	
Blankets, sheets, etc	
Drapes, rugs & linoleum	
Dishes, glasses, silverware	
Appliances bought or repaired	
Garden equipment	
HOUSING TOTAL	$

House & furniture	
Health	
Life	
INSURANCE TOTAL	$

Doctor	
Dentist	
Eyeglasses	
Medicines	
Vitamins	
MEDICAL TOTAL	$

Payments on loans	
Extra debt reduction	
Other	
MISCELLANEOUS TOTAL	$

Baby sitting	
Cameras and film	
Entertainment	
Hobbies & games	
Pets and their upkeep	
TV purchase & repair	
Sporting equipment	
Toys, play equipment	
Vacations	
RECREATION/VACATION TOTAL	$

Income tax deposits	
Property taxes	
TAXES/LICENSES/FEES TOTAL	$

Christmas cards, gifts, decorations	
Flowers as gifts, funerals	
Gifts to friends	
GIFTS/CHRISTMAS TOTAL	$

Airline fares	
Bus and taxi fares	
Car payments	
Car repair & licenses	
Gasoline & oil	
Car insurance	
TRANSPORTATION TOTAL	$

*** SAVINGS TOTAL**	$

**** TOTAL CATEGORIES**	$

* Place an asterisk (*) by the amount under the category you wish to put in savings each month. Total these amounts and put the total in the SAVINGS TOTAL category.

** The total on this line has to be <u>less</u> than your take-home pay.

SAVING SUMMARY FORM

ACCOUNT NAME:________________________ AMOUNT BUDGETED: $______________

DATE	NAME	DEPOSITED		SPENT		BALANCE	

BUDGET PAYMENT PER PAY PERIOD

Money and the CHRISTIAN

ACCOUNT NAME	PERIOD 1		PERIOD 2		PERIOD 3		PERIOD 4	
Clothing / Cleaning								
Contingency / Allowances								
Education								
Food								
Gifts / Christmas								
Housing								
Insurance								
Medical								
Miscellaneous								
Recreation / Vacation								
Taxes / Licenses / Fees								
Tithes / Contributions								
Transportation								
TO SAVINGS:								
Car Insurance								
Car Repairs								
Clothes								
Contingencies								
Education								
Miscellaneous Savings								
Recreation								
Repairs / Improvements								
Total Expenses								
Net Income Available								
Over / Under (Short)								

CHAPTER 7

HOW TO DEVELOP SALES RESISTANCE

1. Understand the job of a salesperson.

He or she is not a counselor. A salesperson's job is to induce you to buy. He or she is trained to translate the features of a product or service into what you perceive to be personal benefits. Word pictures can be skillfully painted to make you "see" yourself enjoying the benefits.

2. Establish the accuracy of a sales pitch.

Some salespeople may make sweeping claims about their products or services. *It is incumbent upon you to establish the accuracy of these statements.* You must search out the negatives.

Proverbs 14:15

A simple man believes anything, but a prudent man gives thought to his steps.

(New English Bible—"A clever man understands the need for proof.")

The salesperson may say:	The true meaning:
"See how much you will *save*" "For an *investment* of only…" "We offer easy *credit*"	"See how much you will *spend*" "For a true *cost* of…" "We offer easy *debt*"

3. Whether you are using a check or credit card always think of it as real cash.

Sometimes using a check or credit card makes a person underestimate in his or her mind the actual cost of a purchase.

4. Determine your hourly income after the Lord's tithe and taxes, then calculate the cost in hours worked to earn the money for a major purchase.

This exercise should make you comprehend the true cost of the purchase.

5. **Develop a delayed action rule.**

   When making a major purchase, learn to say with resolve, "Thank you, I will let you know within a day or two what the decision is."

   This will allow a husband and wife time to discuss the purchase, without the influence of a third party.

Proverbs 23:23 (TLB)

Get the facts at any price, and hold on tightly to all the good sense you can get.

BEFORE MAKING ANY MAJOR PURCHASE, CONSIDER THE FOLLOWING QUESTIONS:

1. Am I pandering to the human weakness of being discontent?

2. Do I really need the purchase or am I rationalizing in order to buy something I do not need, or do not need right now?

3. Am I a victim of alluring advertising and subtle sales tactics?

   - The lust of the eye (I John 2:15-17)
   - Successful-appearing models

4. Is the price fair?

5. Have I comparison-shopped?

   Go to the public library and check the *Consumer Report* regarding your proposed purchase.

6. Have I investigated the retailer's reputation?

   Sometimes it may be to your advantage to pay a

Hebrews 13:5

...be content with what you have.

Proverbs 12:15

The way of a fool seems right to him, but a wise man listens to advice.

higher price, if the retailer offers support and additional service.

7. Does the Lord say, "Yes"?

   (Also review the questions on page 44.)

   The remainder of this chapter is designed to assist you in your quest for seed. It deals with ways to economize. These suggestions are offered not to make you focus on lack but to help you through the remedial process of bringing kingdom order to your finances.

   The objective is to enable you to cut the cost of living without affecting the standard of living more than is necessary.

   The ultimate goal is two-fold: to enable you to receive increase and to cut your expenses. Initially, as faith is being developed for increase, it is usually easier to cut expenses than to raise your income.

   Often people are unaware how much loss they are experiencing by needlessly overspending. Jesus certainly was not a miser, but after the feeding of the multitude he commissioned his disciples to gather up the fragments. He said, "Let nothing be wasted." (John 6:12)

   Make that a goal of yours—that there be no waste. Have a pencil in hand as you read the following pages and mark the items you feel need attention in your life.

Matthew 26:39

Yet not as I will, but as you will.

299 WAYS TO STRETCH YOUR DOLLARS

A PENNY SAVED IS MORE THAN A PENNY EARNED!

The penny earned is subject to federal income taxes, plus state income taxes, if any, and social security tax. So if you could save $1,000 on a vacation by choosing a near-by-fun-place you can drive to as opposed to, say, flying the family to Hawaii, it would be the equivalent of having to have earned $1,400 or $1,500.

FOOD

____ 1. Never go shopping without a thoughtfully prepared list.

____ 2. Consider gasoline costs before driving all over town for advertised bargains.

____ 3. Try to go grocery shopping no more than once a week.

____ 4. To avoid temptation to buy on impulse, shop when you are not hungry.

____ 5. Shop when the store is less crowded (Thursday nights or early Saturday mornings).

____ 6. Invest in an inexpensive credit-card-sized calculator to use while shopping.

____ 7. Keep a running total of purchases in the memory of the calculator.

____ 8. Buy the staples first, and keep track on the calculator. You will probably buy fewer extras if you know how much you've already spent.

____ 9. Use the calculator to determine the unit price of items priced in multiples, such as 4 cans for $1.39.

____ 10. Use the calculator to compare the cost per ounce of different sizes.

____ 11. Calculate the cost per serving when buying meats and costly fruits.

____ 12. Watch the prices of items as they are being scanned into the cash register. Often you can catch costly mistakes. Some stores offer the item free when the scanner overcharges for it.

____ 13. Take advantage of coupon offers only <u>on items you would buy anyway.</u>

____ 14. Avoid buying unneeded products just because you have a coupon.

____ 15. Consider shopping at stores that offer "double couponing."

____ 16. Clip coupons for the brands you normally use from your local newspaper. Coupons are usually published in the Thursday morning and Sunday editions of the newspaper.

____ 17. If a store has run out of an advertised special, ask for a rain check.

____ 18. If possible, shop alone. Leaving children with a friend alleviates pressure to buy unnecessary items.

____ 19. Avoid junk foods, processed foods and convenience foods, not only for your health's sake but for the sake of your pocketbook. Doing this can cut 10% or more from your total grocery bill.

____ 20. Check out the "no-frill" supermarkets where you can save by packing your own groceries and buying products displayed in their original cartons.

____ 21. Make and freeze your own TV dinners from leftovers.

____ 22. Consider "house brands" as opposed to the more costly name brands.

____ 23. Check the lower shelves. More expensive items are usually displayed at eye level.

____ 24. Avoid products in a cyclical price hike—for example, melons in February.

____ 25. Consider growing a garden.

____ 26. Learn to can or freeze fruits and vegetables.

____ 27. Buy directly from the farmer or from a farmer's market.

____ 28. Join or organize a food co-op or buying club.

____ 29. Use a blender to prepare "homemade" baby foods.

____ 30. Non-grocery items purchased at the grocery store might be purchased less expensively elsewhere.

____ 31. Enjoy better health and save money by eating less meat.

____ 32. Turkey is less expensive and contains less fat than beef or pork.

____ 33. Take a lunch to work or school instead of eating out.

____ 34. Measure the cost of eating out in terms of its yearly expense. If you spend $5 for lunch plus a beverage and tip each working day, multiply, say $7, by five days a week times fifty-two weeks. Each year you will spend $1,820 for lunches. This exercise will help give proper attention to seemingly inconsequential expenses.

____ 35. Minimize the drinking of bottled or canned soft drinks. Flavor water with fruit juice or powdered mixes. Learn to enjoy water.

____ 36. Buy bread and baked goods from bakery thrift outlets.

____ 37. For snacks, use carrots, celery and other fresh vegetables and fruits.

____ 38. Eat at home regularly.

____ 39. Eat at restaurants only for special occasions.

____ 40. Consider that the cost of a restaurant meal is at least 10%-20% more than the menu price because of tipping requirements and sales tax.

____ 41. Avoid restaurants with a large, specialized staff, each of whom must be tipped separately.

____ 42. Some cafeterias have a "mini-plate" consisting of a half-portion of meat, two vegetables and a bread at an economical price. Traditionally, there are no tipping requirements in most cafeterias.

____ 43. Look for two-for-one coupons for restaurant dining in your newspapers and mailers.

____ 44. Cut down on the use of paper napkins, towels and other disposables.

____ 45. Don't throw away a spoiled product that you have just bought. Return it to the store for a refund.

____ 46. Avoid the high cost of bottled water by investing in a quality water filter.

____ 47. Planning means saving. Plan menus around advertised and seasonal specials.

Seasonal buying guide:

Fruits	*Peak season*
Apples	September - March
Apricots	June - July
Blueberries	July
Cantaloupes	June - August
Cherries	June - July
Cranberries	September - December
Figs	June - October
Grapefruit	October - May
Peaches	July - August
Pears	July - October
Plums	May - September
Raspberries	July
Strawberries	April - June
Watermelons	June - August

Vegetables	
Artichokes	March - May
Asparagus	April - May
Beets	June - October
Broccoli	October - April
Brussels sprouts	September - February
Cauliflower	October
Corn	May - September
Okra	June - August
Peas	May - September
Sweet potatoes	September - December
Tomatoes	May - August

ENERGY

____ 1. Have your local power company perform a free energy analysis.

____ 2. Turn off lights and appliances when not being used.

____ 3. Make sure your attic is adequately insulated. If your house does not already have insulation in the outside walls, it is usually not cost effective to add insulation to them now.

____ 4. If you live in the South, consider adding a radiant shield barrier in your attic.

____ 5. Consider installing a wind turbine or an electric roof ventilator.

____ 6. Set hot water heater to a moderate setting (120°).

____ 7. Wrap the water heater with a fiberglass insulation kit.

____ 8. Periodically drain the water heater from the bottom drain to remove sediments.

____ 9. Repair leaky faucets, especially on the hot water side.

____ 10. Read your utility bills and check meters for accuracy.

____ 11. Take a shower instead of a bath. This can save up to half the total hot water used in a household.

____ 12. Buy a water-restriction shower head, that gives you plenty of water without waste.

____ 13. If away from your home more than three days, turn off the water heater.

____ 14. Insulate hot water pipes.

____ 15. Make sure the dishwasher is full before running it.

____ 16. Open dishwasher after the rinse cycle, so dishes can air dry.

____ 17. Periodically vacuum dust from the refrigerator and freezer coils.

____ 18. When washing clothes, adjust water level for partial loads or make sure you wash with a full load.

____ 19. Keep the lint filter clean on your dryer to save energy.

____ 20. Use the solar-powered dryer (the clothesline) when possible.

____ 21. When buying a new appliance, consider the yellow and black *Energy Guide* label that tells the approximate cost to operate for one year.

____ 22. Change the bag on the vacuum cleaner frequently for more efficient use.

____ 23. Turn televisions off when not viewing.

____ 24. Repair leaky toilets.

____ 25. Fill a quart plastic milk bottle with water and put it in the tank of the commode. This fills the space and less water is used to flush.

____ 26. Water the lawn only once a week. Give one inch per week in the early morning hours.

____ 27. Use sealer tape to seal window air leaks.

____ 28. Consider installing storm windows and doors.

____ 29. When you must replace a furnace or an air conditioner, consider buying a heat pump high efficiency system.

____ 30. Close the damper on the fireplace when it is not in use.

____ 31. Wear a sweater in the winter and adjust thermostat accordingly.

____ 32. With a sweater, 68° is just as comfortable as 72°. In cold climates such an adjustment will lower the fuel consumption by 12%.

____ 33. Wear cool cotton in the summer.

____ 34. By setting the thermostat at 78° rather than 72°, home cooling costs will be reduced as much as 40%-50% in hot climates.

____ 35. Consider an automatic setback thermostat.

____ 36. Use electric blankets instead of high nighttime settings of the thermostat.

____ 37. Close all vents in unused rooms.

____ 38. Keep furnace filters clean.

____ 39. Make sure drapes or furniture are not blocking heating or cooling outlets.

____ 40. Consider installing a solar water heating device. A $500-$1,000 investment can save $200 per year. This is a 20%-40% tax-free return.

____ 41. Use smaller appliances such as a microwave or a toaster oven instead of heating up the big oven.

____ 42. Plant deciduous trees (trees that lose their leaves in winter) on the west, south, and east sides of your house. The shade from the leaves will protect the house from the summer sun, and in the winter, the warm sunshine will help heat the house.

____ 43. Consider installing a reflective film on west windows.

TELEPHONE

____ 1. Before placing a long distance call, check to see if the business has a toll-free number by calling 1-800-555-1212.

____ 2. Dial direct, as a general rule.

____ 3. Make personal calls during cheaper off-hours, like nighttime or weekends.

____ 4. Consider writing a letter instead of calling.

____ 5. Always get credit for mis-dialed numbers and cutoffs.

____ 6. Keep a written long-distance log, registering the date, time and duration of each long-distance call.

____ 7. Check your long-distance bill carefully. Contest any calls you did not place.

____ 8. If you do not have a service offering a flat rate, compare the rates to cities you frequently call and choose a long-distance company that offers the best rate and service.

____ 9. Choose a long distance service that bills in six-second increments.

____ 10. Choose a calling card that does not charge a per call surcharge and bills in six second increments. Avoid prepaid calling cards which are usually more expensive.

MEDICAL

____ 1. Believe God for divine health.

____ 2. Practice preventive medicine.

____ 3. Maintain a lean body weight.

____ 4. Drink plenty of liquid. (1/2 oz. per lb. of body weight per day)

____ 5. Eat nutritiously with no more than 10%-20% of your total calories from fat.

____ 6. Develop a regular aerobic exercise habit of at least three times per week with a minimum of 20 to 30 minutes duration each.

____ 7. Maintain a positive mental attitude of faith, expecting health and vitality.

____ 8. Choose a good doctor *before* an emergency arises.

____ 9. Choose a doctor who practices preventative medicine.

____ 10. Other than checkups, see a doctor only when absolutely necessary. Get a physical

examination at least once every three years. Some studies indicate that nearly 60% of all hospitalizations could be avoided by early detection and treatment.

____ 11. Choose a doctor who will allow you to discuss minor health problems with himself or herself over the phone.

____ 12. When you must see a doctor, do exactly what he or she tells you.

____ 13. Ask your doctor to prescribe generic drugs rather than the name-brand drugs.

____ 14. Buy private label over-the-counter drugs. Read ingredients. Aspirin is aspirin, no matter how fancy the label.

____ 15. Call several pharmacies before having a prescription filled. Such comparison shopping can save a significant amount. If you must take medication on a regular basis, explore using a reputable mail-order drug company.

____ 16. Ask your doctor for some free samples of your medication.

____ 17. When choosing a hospital, shop around. They do not all charge the same.

____ 18. Insist on an itemized cost breakdown, not just "medical expenses."

____ 19. Reduce hospital bills by requesting that routine tests be conducted prior to admission.

____ 20. Explore the possibility of day surgery.

____ 21. Many unnecessary operations are performed. Get a second opinion.

____ 22. Get children's inoculations at the county health department. Call your city or county health office to find out where you can get such medical procedures done for free.

____ 23. Have your blood pressure checked and keep it under control.

____ 24. Have your cholesterol level checked and keep it under 200.

____ 25. Shop around to find a good dentist. Talk to him or her about fees before the work is done.

CAR EXPENSE

____ 1. Walk or ride a bicycle for close-by errands. The best way to save gas is to not use it at all.

____ 2. Plan errands and do several things in one trip.

____ 3. Check tire pressure regularly. Under-inflated tires waste fuel and accelerate tire wear.

____ 4. When tires need replacing, buy radial tires. They increase the miles per gallon (mpg) and last longer than conventional tires. Look for "take-off" tires from a dealer. Many times purchasers of a new car will install a preferred brand of tires on it and the dealer may sell the take-off tires at a substantial discount. Sometimes you can buy seconds with only cosmetic blemishes at a greatly reduced price.

____ 5. Make sure your wheels are properly aligned and balanced for extended wear and fuel economy.

____ 6. Purchase discount gas from a self-service station that sells quality gasoline. Do not use higher octane than your car requires.

____ 7. Avoid jackrabbit starts. Drive smoothly and steadily. Imagine that an egg is between your foot and the gas pedal. Or, imagine a full glass of water is on the hood and the challenge is to drive without spilling it.

____ 8. Do not exceed the speed limit.

____ 9. Using the air conditioner on your car reduces the MPG by up to four miles per gallon. However, operating your vehicle at freeway speeds with all windows open reduces MPG (because of wind drag) about the same as using the air conditioner.

____ 10. Do not excessively idle a cold engine. All this accomplishes is the burning of gasoline at zero MPG. Except in extremely cold conditions, drive off immediately, maintaining moderate speeds until the engine is warm.

____ 11. Remove unnecessary weight from the trunk.

____ 12. Learn to do minor car repairs and maintenance yourself.

____ 13. Use a good grade motor oil that extends motor life and MPG.

____ 14. Purchase oil, filters, etc. on sale or from a discount distributor.

____ 15. Find a skilled mechanic who will "moonlight" by working on your car during his off hours. Explore bartering for the services.

____ 16. On major repairs, get a firm estimate before authorizing the work. Consider a second opinion.

____ 17. Don't let a good car become an old car. Follow regular maintenance recommendations.

____ 18. Keep your cars clean and waxed. This reduces the temptation to buy a new car.

____ 19. Keep a log of regular maintenance and repairs. It will help you get top dollar at the time of resale.

____ 20. Consider getting rid of a second or third car.

____ 21. Take advantage of car pooling. See if your city government has an agency to assist in the creation of car pool units.

PURCHASING A CAR

____ 1. Drive the best car you can afford until you can afford to pay cash for the car you want.

____ 2. The cheapest car you can own is usually the paid-for car you presently own.

____ 3. Repairs on your present car are usually less than the car payments on a new one.

____ 4. If you must get another car, consider buying a late-model, low-mileage, well-maintained used car. The average depreciation of a new car during the first year is 31.5% of its purchase price. A three or four-year-old car can sometimes be purchased for 50% of the cost of a new car.

____ 5. Try to talk to the previous owner of a used car before you buy it.

____ 6. Ask a bank officer to look at his or her up-to-date used car price book that lists the wholesale and retail prices of all cars. Attempt to pay no more than $100 over the wholesale price, if possible.

____ 7. Thoroughly inspect a used car before buying. Pay a knowledgeable mechanic to check it out thoroughly for you. As a rule, be leery of a car that has been repainted. Look for rust.

____ 8. Be willing to accept minor repairs on a used car if they will help you secure a substantial price reduction.

____ 9. Negotiate for a short-term 100% guarantee on a used car, if possible.

____ 10. When trading cars, clean and wax your old car and sell it by advertising in the newspaper rather than using it as a trade-in.

____ 11. Buy the smallest car that will fit your needs.

____ 12. If you must finance a car, consider your bank or credit union before you finance a car through a dealership.

____ 13. If you must purchase a new car, purchase only options you really use.

____ 14. If you must finance a car, avoid being pressured into purchasing credit life insurance. It is expensive and unnecessary if you have adequate life insurance.

____ 15. Shop around for the best new car deal. Year-end closeouts and demonstrators are greatly reduced toward the end of the year.

____ 16. Check with the *Consumer's Report* for the best buys, as well as models to avoid.

____ 17. Save money by buying through a car broker. Check with American Automobile Brokers, Inc., 24001 Southfield Rd., Suite 110, Southfield, MI 48075, (810) 569-5900 (Their

area code is slated to change mid 1997. If this number does not work, consult information.) Call them for information about how to get a free quote. Shop your local dealers, then get a quote from American. Also call Car/Puter International Corporation (800) 221-4001 for information about how they can save you money.

AIR TRAVEL

____ 1. Purchase tickets ahead of time. You can save as much as 60% off standard fares by planning ahead.

____ 2. Read *The Airline Passenger's Guerrilla Handbook* by George Grown (Blake Publishing Group) to learn legal ways you can get around the airline's multitiered fare system.

____ 3. Find a good travel agent who will search out the best fare available at the time of booking.

____ 4. Join a travel club that will give you a cash rebate of 3% to 5% on domestic flights.

____ 5. Watch the papers for ads from the discount airlines such as Southwest, America West, Hawaiian and Midway. They offer spectacular savings for advance purchases but there is no flexibility. Expiration dates, limitations on refunds and exchanges are strictly enforced.

____ 6. Some airlines can only fly to adjoining states because of federal regulation. Buy a ticket to a city in an adjoining state and then purchase another ticket to your final destination. To satisfy legal requirements, you may not be able to take the next scheduled flight out. You may have to wait for the second flight to your destination.

____ 7. Split the ticket. Say you want to fly round-trip from New York to Los Angeles and the fare is $500. You find that the fare to Las Vegas via Northwest is only $265 round-trip. Then you buy a round-trip ticket from Las Vegas to Los Angeles on America West for $115. You save $120.

____ 8. Buy two round-trip tickets. If you must travel during the week, you will have to pay more because you miss the lower Saturday stay-over fares. Your strategy is to buy two round-trip

tickets, each with a Saturday stay-over. Use the first leg of the first ticket on say, Monday and the first leg of the second ticket when you return on say, Friday. Throw the other tickets away and save around 18%.

____ 9. Buy a ticket on the midnight flight ("red-eye" special) for big savings. Show up at the airport for an earlier flight and tell the agent at the gate you would like to take the earlier flight if there is a seat available. Most airlines will honor your discounted ticket on a standby basis.

____ 10. Check out discounts for senior citizens, children, students, military, clergy, etc.

____ 11. Volunteer to get bumped if your flight is one typically over-booked. Federal law requires that the airline compensate confirmed passengers who are bumped. That usually means travel to their destination plus an additional free flight or a cash voucher for use on an airline ticket from the issuer.

____ 12. If you travel a lot, join the frequent-flier program. Frequent-flier points are worth about two cents a mile.

CLOTHING

____ 1. Before shopping for new clothes, look through your closet and inventory the wardrobe. There may be wearable garments which only need repairing, altering and/or cleaning.

____ 2. Clean out the closet of all clothing you no longer wear. If the items are in good condition, donate them to the Salvation Army or other charitable groups for a tax receipt.

____ 3. Buy new clothes in washable fabrics.

____ 4. If sewing is enjoyable, it can be economical especially for children's clothing.

____ 5. Use proper care in maintaining your clothes and shoes. Be sure they are clean before storing for the season.

____ 6. Use coin-operated dry cleaning machines for sweaters, drapes, etc. instead of commercial cleaners.

____ 7. Use Woolite or a liquid dishwater soap for sweaters. Lay them out flat to air dry. Do not put sweaters in the dryer.

____ 8. Buy your clothes on sale.

____ 9. Buy clothes in off-seasons.

____ 10. Explore factory outlets and so-called underground shopping warehouses that carry unmarked name-brand goods.

____ 11. Use wood "shaped" hangers for tailored garments. Hang them up immediately after taking them off and allow them to air out before putting them into the closet.

____ 12. Pay attention to the care instructions on the label.

____ 13. Avoid damage from over-drying.

____ 14. Buy children's clothes with ample room for growth.

____ 15. Don't be embarrassed to explore the possibility of buying quality, clean, used clothing from a thrift store or a garage sale.

____ 16. Change out of expensive church or business clothing before cooking or lounging at home.

____ 17. Do not buy clothing on credit.

____ 18. Select outfits that can be mixed and used in multiple combinations rather than only as a single unit.

____ 19. Trade your children's clothes with friends who have children.

____ 20. Choose traditional styles, especially in men's suiting. Choose all wool or wool blends in conservative dark colors to maximize the wearing opportunity and garment life.

____ 21. Always buy quality material and workmanship.

____ 22. Avoid fads.

FURNITURE & APPLIANCES

____ 1. Buy from classified ads and garage sales. Due to people breaking up housekeeping, being transferred, etc., quality used furniture and appliances can usually be purchased at significant savings.

____ 2. If buying an appliance new, avoid the deluxe models. Normally the extra knobs and buttons cost far more than they are worth and some features are seldom if ever used. Besides, extra features mean more things that can break down.

____ 3. Avoid dealer service contracts. If you do purchase one, be sure it is not duplicating your manufacturer's warranty.

____ 4. Use a credit card such as a gold card that offers double manufacturers' warranties when purchasing electronics or appliances.

____ 5. Buy a home maintenance and repair book. Before calling in a repair man, check the manual to see if it is a minor repair you can make.

____ 6. Check the *Consumer Report* for comparisons of different models.

____ 7. Always shop around. Try to buy wholesale. Check with mail order houses. Don't buy in a hurry.

____ 8. For insurance purposes, make a complete pictorial or video inventory and identify all your belongings before you have a loss from fire or theft.

MEDICAL INSURANCE

____ 1. The cheapest health insurance is probably the free plan your employer may provide.

____ 2. Take advantage of group policies. Rates are usually better if you can be included in a group.

____ 3. Be aware that many group policies charge an additional monthly administration fee per individual and require you to purchase their life insurance policy for a specified death benefit amount. Consider the total cost when you comparison shop.

____ 4. If you must provide your own insurance, get insurance from an A+ or A rated company that specializes in health care. Check the rating in the *Best's Insurance Reports* at the library.

____ 5. Shop around for the best rates for the same coverage. Be sure to compare apples with apples. Rates can vary as much as $1,200 a year or more per person.

____ 6. Before buying the insurance, check on the company's history of rate increases. Rate increases can boost rates up 25% or more.

____ 7. Understand that health insurance covers two areas: (1) major medical for in-hospital care, and (2) outpatient care. The major need for insurance is for the catastrophic illness.

____ 8. Analyze whether it is cost efficient to pay higher premiums for full outpatient benefits.

____ 9. A large portion of the premium you pay is paid to insure the first $1,000. See what would happen to your rates if you raise the deductible to $1,000 on the major medical portion. Even if you have an occasional out-of-pocket expense, the big savings on premiums may save you money in the long run. If you feel uncomfortable self-insuring the first $1,000, you may want to maintain a low-or-no-annual-fee, low-interest credit card to use in such an emergency.

____ 10. Also explore what happens to the premium cost if the outpatient portion of the policy has a higher deductible. Many companies have an accident rider that has no deductible.

____ 11. Get major medical that pays for a second opinion if surgery is indicated.

____ 12. Make sure your coverage allows you to choose your own doctor and hospital.

____ 13. Do not carry duplicate coverage. You can't collect twice for the same illness.

____ 14. Avoid coverage you do not need. Example, maternity benefits at age 50, etc.

____ 15. Buy any new policy before you cancel existing policies to make certain you are still insurable.

____ 16. Make sure you read and understand your policy. Pay special attention to eligible expenses, exclusions and limitations.

____ 17. Avoid those health and life insurance policies hyped on television and through the mail. Often their premiums are 400% too high.

____ 18. If you are forced to pay for your own health insurance costs, consider Good Samaritan Group. They are a nontraditional program created for Christians to "bear one anothers' burdens." It may provide the protection you need at a reduced cost. Their address and telephone number is: The Good Samaritan Program, P.O. Box 279, Beech Grove, Indiana 46107 (317) 894-2000.

LIFE INSURANCE

____ 1. Reconsider the wisdom of buying life insurance on children. The purpose of life insurance is to protect against the loss of financial assets.

____ 2. As your responsibilities decrease, consider carrying less life insurance.

____ 3. If you are single with no dependents, reconsider your need for life insurance.

____ 4. Buy insurance for protection of assets and security for dependents, not as an investment.

____ 5. For the most inexpensive coverage, buy annually-renewable term insurance without any "frills."

____ 6. Shop for the best rate. Costs may vary as much as 300%.

____ 7. If you know exactly what term coverage you want, use a quoting service to find the best rate. Ask about 10-year, 15-year and 20-year level premium plans. For free quotes, call:

InsuranceQuote	800-972-1104
SelectQuote	800-343-1985
TermQuote	800-444-8376

____ 8. If you feel you need assistance from an insurance broker, select one who represents more than one company, preferably one who is a Charter Life Underwriter (CLU). He or she can analyze your situation and help you determine what will serve you best. Ask him or her about variable universal life and other options available.

____ 9. Avoid companies with a rating of less than A in the *Best's Insurance Report* at your library.

____ 10. Avoid a company unless it will allow you to renew without proof of continued good health until at least 65 to 70.

____ 11. Consider the wisdom of switching companies every few years. Many companies offer the first five years of annual renewable term insurance at less than competitive rates. Consider changing every five years to take advantage of a new set of lower rates.

____ 12. Buy any new policy before you cancel existing policies to make certain you are still insurable.

____ 13. Explore replacing your existing whole life and universal life policies with term life. Reinvest the premium difference in mutual funds, variable annuities or other good investments. A 35-year-old man, a nonsmoker in good health, can provide $250,000 of coverage for as little as $180 the first year. Premiums would be ten times that amount for the same coverage from a whole life policy. The cost for the term policy would not exceed the whole life premium for many, many years. By that time, the need for insurance may have decreased.

____ 14. If you have been paying for a whole-life policy for many years, don't just drop it; see if it can be converted to some type of paid-up policy.

____ 15. Explore the possibility of borrowing against a whole-life insurance policy at 5 or 6% if you already have built up a large cash value.

____ 16. As you become debt-free, and/or when your children are grown and self-supporting and/or you have a substantial net worth, consider reducing or even dropping coverage.

____ 17. Avoid insurance-by-mail schemes.

HOMEOWNER INSURANCE

____ 1. At renewal time, comparison shop for the best rates.

____ 2. For significant savings consider coverage with $500, $1,000 or 1% deductible.

____ 3. Take only the coverage you need. Generally the Broad Form is all that is needed.

____ 4. Be aware that most homeowner policies do not cover flood damage but will cover damage caused by frozen pipes.

____ 5. Homeowner insurance does not usually include glass breakage, earthquake damage, settling problems or certain expensive items such as personal computers and jewelry.

____ 6. Read the fine print on your policy. Understand all coverage limitations and the amounts covered. Make sure all the personal property you want covered is covered at replacement value.

____ 7. Purchase a rider policy to cover any items excluded from your policy that you feel need to be covered such as personal computers, jewelry and other articles.

____ 8. Have flood insurance coverage only if you are in a government-designated floodplain or if

your mortgage company requires it.

____ 9. Carry fire insurance of at least but not more than 90% of the replacement cost (not including land) of your home. Do not over-insure because you are paying premium dollars for something you can never collect.

____ 10. If you rent, get a tenant's policy to insure contents and personal belongings.

AUTO INSURANCE

____ 1. Choose the right company. Rates vary significantly.

____ 2. Reduce collision and comprehensive costs by selecting the right car. Check with your agent before buying the car.

____ 3. Cut the comprehensive and collision coverage of an older car. The insurance company won't pay more to repair a car than it is worth. Each year's depreciation diminishes the maximum claim you can make against your collision coverage.

____ 4. Be aware of service charges and/or interest when paying installments on premiums.

____ 5. Do not list a young person as the *principal* driver of a car if you can legally and in good faith do so.

____ 6. Maintain a good driving record. If you were given a ticket unjustly, fight it.

____ 7. If practical, use the least expensive car as the one you use to commute to work.

____ 8. Consider car pooling.

____ 9. Use public transportation to commute to work and thus reduce rates.

____ 10. Drop duplicate protection. You may already be covered by health insurance and you may

therefore consider dropping the personal injury protection (PIP). You may not need the uninsured motorist option if your family has a good group medical insurance policy. (If your vehicle is hit by an uninsured motorist, your collision insurance will pay for the damages to your car, subject to your deductible.) CAUTION: You may have some exposure for non-family members riding in your car who do not have insurance.

____ 11. Take a higher deductible. Raise the deductible on collision and on your comprehensive for significant savings.

____ 12. Ask for and receive discounts. If you have installed an antitheft device you may qualify for a discount.

____ 13. Young drivers completing a driver's education course, multi-car families, age group of 50 to 64, senior citizens, certain professions including the military or if you use the same company for your homeowner's insurance—all may qualify for discounts. Ask.

GIFTS

____ 1. Get in the habit of buying gifts throughout year. January clearance sales are not too soon to start buying for next Christmas.

____ 2. Set a dollar limit per gift and stick to it.

____ 3. Buy Christmas wrap and cards in January at substantial discounts.

____ 4. Make as many gifts as you can. Such crafts are a meaningful yet inexpensive gift.

____ 5. Don't charge gifts. You will be tempted to go over a preset dollar limit.

VACATIONS & RECREATION

____ 1. Look for alternatives to spending money on recreation. For example, consider going to the zoo or to a public beach instead of a high-cost amusement park.

____ 2. Plan vacations during the reduced rate "off-seasons."

____ 3. Rather than going out for the evening, plan a family night of barbecue, popcorn, games, etc.

____ 4. Instead of taking friends to an expensive restaurant, and spending $50-$100 or more, prepare a meal at home for much less and enjoy it more. Hospitality is becoming a lost art.

____ 5. When traveling by car, eat at least one meal at a roadside picnic area instead of a restaurant.

____ 6. Consider the economy of renting a boat or a motorhome when desired as opposed to the high cost of ownership (insurance, depreciation, loss of earning on tied-up capital, etc.).

CREDIT

____ 1. Use great caution in borrowing for anything. Remember that the Bible discourages debt.

____ 2. Make certain that the benefits of borrowing *far* exceed the cost of the loan.

____ 3. Never, ever borrow for an impulse item. Use a charge card for extended credit only after prayerful thought considering all the consequences.

____ 4. Make sure what you are purchasing will last longer than it takes to pay for it.

____ 5. Avoid the double jeopardy of purchasing depreciable items on credit.

____ 6. The Bible discourages co-signing. Do so only if you are willing and able to pay the debt of someone else. You will probably have to.

____ 7. Use charge cards only if you can pay off the entire amount during the grace period thereby avoiding all interest costs.

____ 8. Call or write Bankcard Holders of America, 524 Branch Drive, Salem, Virginia 24153, (703) 917 9805 to get a list of the credit cards offering the best rates. There is a nominal fee for this service.

____ 9. When looking for the best card, take advantage of the NEW FEDERAL FAIR CREDIT and CHARGE CARD DISCLOSURE ACT. It requires all credit card solicitations to include a uniform table that discloses: (1) annual percentage rate, (2) annual fee, (3) minimum finance charge, (4) grace period, (5) transaction fee, and (6) method used for calculating the balance.

____ 10. Use your card as a bargaining tool. If you are dealing directly with the owner of a retail establishment, he or she may agree to grant you a discount, say 5%, if you agree ***not*** to use your charge card. The merchant may agree to the discount so that he or she will not have to pay a fee to the bank. It is a win-win situation. You won't know until you ask.

____ 11. Do not borrow money at interest rates of 10% to 21% when you have a savings account earning interest at much lower rates.

____ 12. Do not overwithhold. If you are getting a refund, you are giving the government an interest-free loan. Ask your employer to help you fill out a W-4 form and claim on it the number of allowances that will enable you to reduce the amount withheld from the paycheck in order to break even with the IRS at the end of each year.

____ 13. Try to earn interest on all liquid assets.

____ 14. Deposit all income into an interest-bearing account as soon as possible.

____ 15. If you must borrow, shop for the most inexpensive money you can find.

____ 16. If you experience payment problems, go immediately to the lender and explain the situation and work out an agreeable arrangement. Most cities have nonprofit credit counseling agencies to help you work out a plan. To locate one near you, call the

Consumer Credit Counseling Service (1-800-388-2227).

____ 17. If you purchase with an installment contract, read and understand all provisions of the contract.

SHELTER

____ 1. When buying a house, look for three things: (1) a well-located, well-maintained neighborhood where houses are appreciating in value, (2) if possible, assumable low-interest financing, and (3) a seller willing to sell at a price below market.

____ 2. Consider the purchase of an older home you can improve with your own labor.

____ 3. If you feel you will be relocating to a different geographical region within three years or less, consider renting instead of buying. In a soft market, houses generally will not appreciate enough to cover the high cost of closing on another one in less than four years.

____ 4. Do your own lawn care, spraying and pest control.

MISCELLANEOUS

____ 1. Shop around for the best rate on your savings. Check money market bank accounts, CDs, money market mutual funds, credit unions, etc.

____ 2. Choose a bank that offers both good service and low or no service charges on your personal account.

____ 3. When possible avoid or minimize commissions of all kinds.

____ 4. Consider using discount stock brokers.

____ 5. Consider no-load mutual funds directly from the investment companies.

____ 6. Buy or sell real estate directly when possible.

____ 7. Buy merchandise directly from the manufacturer or wholesale distributor when possible.

____ 8. For financial reasons as well as health, give up smoking and drinking.

____ 9. Try to make major purchases during sales.

January	Holiday clearances and white sales
February	Washington and Lincoln's birthday sales; winter clearances
March	Winter sports equipment sales
April	After Easter clothing sales and canned goods sales
May	Memorial Day sales on garden and vacation items
June	Frozen food sales
July	Fourth of July sales
August	Back-to-school sales
September	Home improvement sales, pre-holiday sales and end-of-year car sales
October	Veteran's Day sales
November & December	Worst months to buy anything. <u>Get December Christmas shopping done before the end of October.</u>

____ 10. If you are paying Private Mortgage Insurance (PMI) as part of your monthly house payment and you have a loan-to-value ratio of 80% or less, often the mortgage company may not require continuation of the PMI. Determine if this is the case and work with your mortgage company to get the coverage dropped.

CHAPTER 8

INVESTING

DON'T CONSIDER INVESTING UNTIL...

An investment program to meet long-term goals should be begun only after the following steps have been taken:

1. You are tithing faithfully and consistently.

You cannot invest money to inure to your benefit that does not belong to you in the first place. That would be fraud and embezzlement.

2. All consumer debt has been paid off.

The money used to pay off high-interest debt, yields greater dividends than most investments. Furthermore, it is a risk-free and tax-free yield.

3. A rapid reduction program is in place for long-term debt.

This program should involve all long-term debt with interest rates of 9½% or greater—such as debts on real estate, cars, R.Vs., etc. Often, a home, held for a long period of time, not only provides shelter for the family and ministry to others through hospitality, but it can be a sound investment. Set a goal to own your home free-and-clear as soon as possible.

Ecclesiastes 3:1

There is a time for everything, and a season for every activity.

Ecclesiastes 8:6

For there is a proper time and procedure for every matter.

Malachi 3:8

Will a man rob God?

4. One month's living expenses are in your checking account.

This will eliminate NSF checks and give some flexibility and "breathing room" so you won't be living 48 hours from insolvency.

5. An emergency reserve has been established in a money market fund.

Not having a reserve fund of at least two to three months' income causes many to terminate their investment plan prematurely if an unforeseen emergency arises. The purpose of an emergency fund is to provide peace-of-mind knowing you have a cushion against unforeseen *minor* problems. The *major* crises will be covered by major medical, disability, auto and home insurance.

A money market mutual fund account is ideal for the emergency reserve because you can write checks on it if the need arises.

Proverbs 22:3

A prudent man foresees the difficulties ahead and prepares for them; the simpleton goes blindly on and suffers the consequences.

Proverbs 21:20

In the house of the wise are stores of choice food and oil.

6. A savings program has been established for upcoming major purchases.

This is for planned purchases of major items such as an automobile, furniture, a home or the down payment on a home.

GOD APPROVES OF INVESTING

The Parable of the Ten Minas

Compare this parable with the Parable of the Talents found in Matthew 25:14-30. (Note the differences and the similarities.)

- Everything we have comes from God.

- Doing things God's way is contrary to man's way.

- Wise money management pleases the Lord.

- Poor money management displeases the Lord.

- Good results receive a greater reward.

Luke 19:12-26

He said: "A man of noble birth went to a distant country to have himself appointed king and then to return. So he called ten of his servants and gave them ten minas, 'Put this money to work,' he said, 'until I come back.'

"But his subjects hated him and sent a delegation after him to say, 'We don't want this man to be our king.'

"He was made king, however, and returned home. Then he sent for the servants to whom he had given the money, in order to find out what they had gained with it.

"The first one came and said, 'Sir, your mina has earned ten more.'

"'Well done, my good servant!' his master replied. 'Because you have been trustworthy in a very small matter, take charge of ten cities.'

"The second came and said, 'Sir, your mina has earned five more.'

"His master answered, 'You take charge of five cities.'

"Then another servant came and said, 'Sir, here is your mina; I have kept it laid away in a piece of cloth. I was afraid of you, because you are a hard man. You take out what you did not put in and reap what you did not sow.'

"His master replied, 'I will judge you by your own words, you wicked servant! You knew, did you, that I am a hard man, taking out what I did not put in, and reaping what I did not sow? Why then didn't you put my money on deposit, so that when I came back, I could have collected it with interest?'

"Then he said to those standing by, 'Take his mina away from him and give it to the one who has ten minas.'

"'Sir,' they said, 'he already has ten!'

"He replied, 'I tell you that to everyone who has, more will be given, but as for the one who has nothing, even what he has will be taken away.' "

FOUR FALSE REASONS TO INVEST

1. For a life of ease during retirement

There is nothing wrong with setting aside money you have worked for so it can work for you when you cannot. However, God never intended for a man or woman to totally cease labor and have a period of ease.

Genesis 3:19

By the sweat of your brow you will eat your food until you return to the ground, since from it you were taken.

- Being idle and non-productive brings rejection.
- Often, premature death occurs shortly after retirement.
- Jesus warns against a life of idleness. See the Parable of the Rich Fool (Luke 12:18-20).

2. For present security

- Money must not be the Christian's security.
- Your security must be in God and in your personal development to optimize his deposit in you.

Proverbs 11:28

Whoever trusts in his riches will fall.

3. For financial independence

- The world seeks financial *independence.* You must seek financial *freedom.*
- Do not accumulate wealth for the purpose of getting out of the so-called rat race. Satan tempted Eve to want to be her own boss. It is a delusive idea to seek a life that is out from under all authority, devoid of any restrictions or hindrances so that you can live out a selfish dream.

4. To bring happiness

- Money and happiness are not an "either/or" choice.
- Happiness comes from within and is a choice.

GODLY REASONS TO INVEST AND ACCUMULATE WEALTH

1. To do good.

- Money wisely invested can affect you and your loved ones for generations to come.
- Money can be used to print Bibles, support missionary outreaches, feeds orphans, etc. It can also be used to buy illegal drugs, etc.

Luke 12:15

A man's life does not consist in the abundance of his possessions.

Matthew 13:22

The one who received the seed that fell among the thorns is the man who hears the word, but the worries of this life and the *deceitfulness of wealth* choke it, making it unfruitful.

Ecclesiastes 5:11

As goods increase, so do those who consume them.

Matthew 19:23

Then Jesus said to his disciples, "I tell you the truth, it is hard for a rich man to enter the kingdom of heaven."

Ecclesiastes 5:10

Whoever loves money never has money enough; whoever loves wealth is never satisfied with his income. This too is meaningless.

Genesis 12:2

"I will bless you...and you will be a blessing."

Galatians 3:14,29

He redeemed us in order that the blessing given Abraham might come to the Gentiles through Christ Jesus. If you belong to Christ, then you are Abraham's seed, and heirs according to the promise.

- Studies have revealed that the greater the poverty, the greater the incidences of obesity, alcoholism and other forms of drug addiction including cigarettes, and the higher the rate of crime. Counselors agree that more divorces can be traced to money problems than to any other cause. Stress caused by money problems even causes physical illness.

Ecclesiastes 10:19

Money is the answer for everything.

2. To leave an inheritance

An inheritance should be material wealth *as well as* a godly example, life principles, a good name, prayers, etc.

Proverbs 13:22

A good man leaves an inheritance for his children's children, but a sinner's wealth is stored up for the righteous.

II Corinthians 12:14

Children should not have to save up for their parents, but parents for their children.

3. To help provide college or other assistance to children

I Timothy 5:8

If anyone does not provide for his relatives, and especially for his immediate family, he has denied the faith and is worse than an unbeliever.

4. To be able to help support yourself for ministry in later life

5. For a specific opportunity such as a house, a car, etc.

Proverbs 10:5

He who gathers crops in summer is a wise son but he who sleeps during harvest is a disgraceful son.

THINGS MORE VALUABLE THAN MONETARY WEALTH TO BE SOUGHT AFTER

1. **A good name**

   - Never compromise your testimony for gain. You are ambassadors of Christ. (II Corinthians 5:20)

Proverbs 22:1

A good name is more desirable than great riches; to be esteemed is better than silver or gold.

Psalms 23:3

He guides me in the paths of righteousness for his name's sake.

2. **The law, statutes, precepts, commands, fear and ordinances of the Lord**

   (Psalm 19:7-11)

Psalm 19:10

They are more precious than gold, than much pure gold.

Psalm 119:72

The law from your mouth is more precious to me than thousands of pieces of silver and gold.

3. **Wisdom and understanding**

Proverbs 3:13-16

Blessed is the man who finds wisdom, and the man who gains understanding, for she is more profitable than silver and yields better returns than gold. She is more precious than rubies; nothing you desire can compare with her.

4. **Faith**

I Peter 1:7

These have come so that your faith—of greater worth than gold...may prove genuine.

5. **Your soul**

Mark 8:36

What good is it for a man to gain the whole world, yet forfeit his soul?

HOW TO CREATE WEALTH

CAUTION

"Though your riches increase do not set your heart on them." (Psalm 62:10)

To build wealth beyond most people's expectations, four things are required:

1. Time
2. Discipline
3. Knowledge
4. A plan

1. TIME—THE MAGIC OF COMPOUNDING

- Even a small amount of money, invested systematically over a long period of time will multiply far beyond most people's fondest expectations.
- It is not only *how much* you save that counts; it's the *interest rate* and *how long* it remains invested that make the big difference.
- The chart on the next page demonstrates how much $100 per month (just $3.29 per day) could become over time.

Proverbs 13:11

He who gathers money little by little makes it grow.

THE POWER OF $3.29 PER DAY!

Years	Total Invested	Accumulative Return			
		5%	10%	15%	20%
10	$12,000	$15,528	$20,485	$27,522	$37,610
15	18,000	26,729	41,447	66,651	111,570
20	24,000	41,103	75,937	149,724	310,965
25	30,000	59,551	132,683	324,353	848,529
30	36,000	83,226	226,049	692,328	2,297,784
35	42,000	113,609	379,664	1,457,718	6,204,932
40	48,000	152,602	632,408	3,101,605	16,738,488
45	54,000	202,644	1,048,250	6,544,503	45,136,640
50	60,000	266,865	1,732,439	13,799,311	121,697,208
55	66,000	349,284	2,858,141	29,086,509	328,102,216
60	72,000	455,058	4,710,269	61,299,407	884,563,952
65	78,000	590,803	7,757,591	129,177,824	2,384,768,178
70	84,000	765,013	12,771,378	272,209,958	6,429,273,974

BEGIN AS EARLY IN LIFE AS POSSIBLE

If a young person places $1,200 per year in an investment yielding an annual compounded tax-free return of 15% between the ages of 20 and 26 (for a total of $8,400 contributed) and never contributes another dime over the next 38 years, when he or she reaches 65, that person will have accumulated a retirement plan worth $2,689,808!

However...

Psalms 90:12

Teach us to number our days.

...if he or she had waited until age 27 to make his or her first contribution, and then contributed $1,200 faithfully for the next 38 years ($45,600 contributed) until age 65 in the same type account, he or she would have a retirement plan valued at $1,612,347. The difference is over $1 million. The most astonishing part is that the person contributing from ages 20 through 26 put in less than one fifth the amount of the person who contributed for 38 years. The time to start is now!

Lamentations 3:27

It is good for a man to bear the yoke while he is young.

THE CONSEQUENCE OF WAITING

An example: a 20-year-old and a 50-year-old have the same goal of having $250,000 at age 65. Each can get a compounded return of 12%. The 20-year-old must save only $11.65 per month but the 50-year-old must save $500.42 per month, nearly 43 times as much!

Jeremiah 8:20

The harvest is past, the summer has ended, and we are not saved.

THE RULE OF "72"

To determine when your invested capital will double, divide 72 by your interest rate.

72 ÷ 5% = 14.4 years
72 ÷ 10% = 7.2 years
72 ÷ 15% = 4.8 years
72 ÷ 20% = 3.6 years
72 ÷ 25% = 2.9 years

IT DOESN'T TAKE MUCH!

Look what could happen if you would just forfeit drinking soft drinks or one or two cups of coffee a day and could invest the $1 a day you save by quitting.

Luke 19:17 (KJV)

...because thou hast been faithful in a very little...

THE POWER OF $1.00 PER DAY!

Years	Total Invested	Accumulative Return			
		5%	10%	15%	20%
10	$3,600	$4,658	$6,145	$8,257	$11,283
20	7,200	12,331	22,781	44,917	93,290
30	10,800	24,968	67,815	207,698	689,335
40	14,400	45,781	189,722	930,482	5,021,546
50	18,000	80,060	519,732	4,139.793	36,509,163

* based upon $30 a month with interest compounded monthly

2. Discipline

- Have the discipline to make your investments a "do not touch" fund. Pretend it is not even there until you do need it for one of the goals you have set.
- You must not eat your seed.
- Reject the consumptive lifestyle that spends it all.

II Timothy 1:7

For God did not give us a spirit of timidity, but a spirit of power, of love and of self-discipline.

- Take this eye-opening quiz:

  Determine the total amount of income you've earned to date by taking your average annual income times the number of years you have worked. Now take the amount you have in savings or in investments and divide it by your total earnings. This will give you the percent of your income you have been able to retain over that period of time. If the percentage is embarrassingly low, you have eaten some or all of your seed and have indulged in a consumptive lifestyle.

- Would you keep a trustee who took every cent you invested with him or her as a salary? Why should the Lord trust you with more if you would consume it all? The important thing is not how much you earn but through discipline how much you are able to keep.

James 4:3

When you ask, you do not receive, because you ask with the wrong motives, that you may spend what you get...

3. Knowledge—Knowing Where and When to Invest

1. Invest in knowledge.

- Take career-advancing seminars. Buy audiocassette and videocassette programs and books.
- Subscribe to *Money Magazine* and *Kiplinger's Personal Finance Magazine.*

  Knowledge minimizes risk.

Proverbs 23:23

Buy the truth and do not sell it; get wisdom, discipline and understanding.

2. Invest in your own business.

For a detailed and comprehensive study of this subject, see *Start Your Own Business: A Christian's Step-by-Step Guide to Successfully Starting and Operating a Profitable Business* by Caleb McAfee. See the order form in the back of this book.

Proverbs 20:14

"It's no good, it's no good!" says the buyer; then off he goes and boasts about his purchase.

Proverbs 16:11 (TLB)

The Lord demands fairness in every business deal. He established this principle.

3. Avoid preying upon other people's misery in order to profit; example—taking advantage of a person during a time of financial stress (foreclosures, etc.).

4. Avoid highly-leveraged, no-money-down real estate schemes.

Instead, look for bargain properties you can acquire for cash or with short-term financing, improve, and sell at a profit or operate as rental properties with ideally little or no debt service.

5. Avoid business partnerships.

Especially avoid partnerships with unbelievers whose lives are not governed by Scriptural financial principles.

II Corinthians 6:14-17

Do not be yoked with unbelievers. For what do righteousness and wickedness have in common? Or what fellowship can light have with darkness?...What does a believer have in common with an unbeliever? Therefore come out from them and be ye separate, says the Lord.

6. Avoid high-risk investments and speculations.

Ecclesiastes 5:13,14,17 (TLB)

There is another serious problem I have seen everywhere—savings are put into risky investments that turn sour, and soon there is nothing left to pass on to one's son. The man who speculates is soon back to where he began—with nothing. This, as I said, is a very serious problem, for all his hard work has been for nothing; he has been working for the wind. It is all swept away. All the rest of his life he is under a cloud—gloomy, discouraged, frustrated and angry.

7. Invest in no-load mutual funds.

Here your money is lumped together with the money of thousands of other people into a gigantic pool. The fund then invests in a diversification of companies thus reducing risk. The word, "*no-load*" means you are buying the security directly from the investment company thus paying no commission to a broker.

- *Small minimum investment*

  Most require an initial contribution of $1,000 to $2,500.

  A few have lower minimums especially in the format of an IRA.

- *Liquidity*

  Your shares can be redeemed at any time at their current asset value. This can be more or less than you originally paid.

- *Automatic reinvestment*

  Most funds will automatically reinvest the dividends earned plus any capital gains that may accrue to your account.

- *Automatic withdrawals*

  Upon request, most funds can be set up as an automatic withdrawal plan from your bank account.

THREE BROAD CATEGORIES OF MUTUAL FUNDS

1. Stock funds

A stock fund uses the investor's money to buy thousands of shares of common stock in usually fifty or more different companies. This gives a high degree of safety because of the diversification involved. These funds are managed by some of the best minds on Wall Street and over the past few years, the better managed funds have experienced spectacular growth. Stock funds perform best when the interest rates are low.

As a general rule we recommend *no-load* funds (funds without a sales commission) or *low-load* funds with sales commissions of 3% or less.

2. Bond funds

When interest rates are high, stock funds will generally not perform well. This is a perfect time to switch to the bond funds. Bond funds invest in corporate debt. These bonds give a fixed rate of return, but this is not the only profit they can give. A bond is a negotiable instrument. This means that you can sell it at any time.

If you buy the bond funds when interest rates are high and *about to come down*, the bond increases in value when interest rates do come down. Conversely, if after you buy shares of a bond fund, the rates go up, the value of the bond diminishes. We generally recommend the no-load variety of bond funds.

3. Money market funds

Money market funds buy short-term debt issues. It is a place to have your capital when neither the stock nor the bond funds are the prudent place to be invested. Here your money is on the sideline where the principal has minimal risk. It can sit there earning a decent, albeit low, rate of interest. Your money is liquid and available when the "perfect" investment presents itself.

TWO FUNDAMENTAL INVESTMENT RULES

Rule #1. There is no investment that is always good.

There is no place you can park your money, forget about it and always have that money earning the highest possible yield year after year.

Rule #2. In every economy there is only one best type of investment in which to have your money invested.

The economy changes constantly, and since it changes, you should change your investment strategy accordingly.

HOW TO HAVE YOUR INVESTMENT AT THE RIGHT PLACE IN EACH ECONOMY

Here is a timing strategy that can have you in the market when it is going up and out of the stock market when everyone else is losing money. It is called "The Money Movement Strategy" developed by Charles J. Givens.* This strategy requires you to watch the prime lending rate, that is, the published rate that the major banks charge their most creditworthy borrowers, and the 30-year Treasury Bond rate. You can find these rates listed in the business sections of local newspapers and in national papers such as the *Wall Street Journal* or *USA Today.*

*For a more detailed study of "The Money Movement Strategy" see ***Wealth Without Risk*** by Charles J. Givens.

There are three directions these two interest rates can take. They can go up, go down or remain stable.

To understand this strategy, divide these two interest rates into three categories:

1. **Low-range**—when the prime rate is below 9½% and the 30-year Treasuries are below 8½%
2. **Mid-range**—when the prime rate is between 9½% and 11½% and the 30-year Treasuries are between 8½% and 10½%
3. **High-range**—when the prime rate is above 11½% and the 30-year Treasuries are above 10½%

- If these rates are in the **low-range** and are remaining stable or dropping, be invested in the no-load stock funds.
- If you see rates start up, sell your shares and invest in the money market funds.
- If the rates are in the **mid-range** and are level or going up, continue to remain safely in the money market funds. If the index rates start to drop and the trend continues downward, you can choose either stock or bond mutual funds and do well.
- If the interest rates are in the **high-range**, the best place to be is the money market funds.
- When you observe the prime rate starting down, that is the perfect time to invest in the bond funds.
- If the two rates give the same message, your whole investment portfolio can be invested as indicated above. However, if these two indexes do not speak in concert, consider investing 50% of your portfolio as one index directs and 50% as the other index directs.

30-Year Treasury Bond Chart for Money Movement Strategy

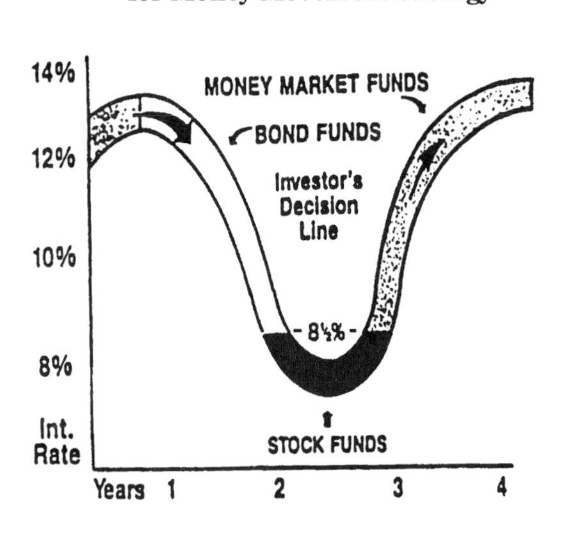

Prime Rate Chart for Money Movement Strategy

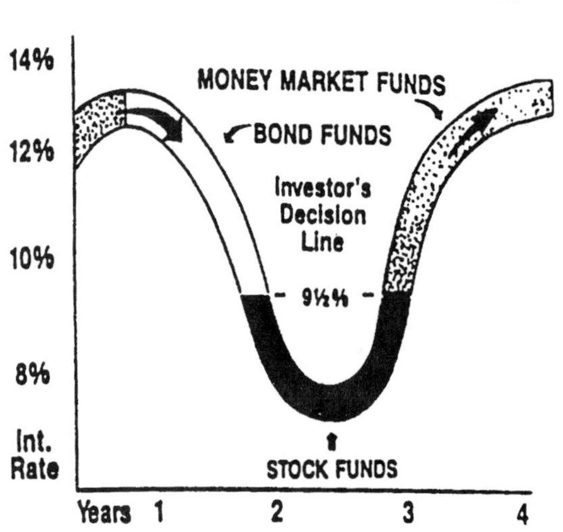

SELECTING A FUND

- Choose a **family of funds**—one that has all three types mentioned in previous pages. The buy/sell transactions mentioned above can be accomplished by a simple telephone call to your fund family.

- Read the section in *Kiplinger's Personal Finance* magazine called "Portfolio Monitor" and the section in *Money Magazine* called "Fund Watch." These sections list the best performing funds. Past performance does not necessarily insure good future performance, but if a fund has consistently done well in a similiar economic climate over an extended period, say five to ten years, it is a safe assumption that management knows what it is doing. The sections in these magazines list the toll-free telephone numbers of the funds. Call several and request their prospectuses.

- Once you choose a fund and invest in it, it is easy to track your investment's performance in the financial section of the paper.

- There are several financial newsletters dealing specifically with mutual fund investing. Some, like *Mutual Fund Forecaster* (800-327-6720), give specific buy and sell recommendations each month. Some public libraries subscribe to financial newsletters.

DOLLAR COST AVERAGING

Some people just don't want to follow any timing strategy no matter how uncomplicated. Here is a workable solution. It is called "dollar cost averaging."
It works as follows:

- You simply commit to buy a fixed dollar amount of a particular mutual fund at regular intervals without regard to its present value.
- When prices are low, of course you will buy more shares than when the net asset value is higher. Consequently, the average per-share-cost is always lower than the simple average of the prices at which the purchases were made.
- Look at this example:

Time Period	Amount Invested	Price Per Share	# Shares Bought
1	$100	$10.00	10.000
2	100	8.00	12.500
3	100	5.00	20.000
4	100	7.00	14.286
5	100	9.00	11.111

In the above example, the $100 is invested regularly each period. The average of the five prices is $7.80. If you figure it up, the $500 invested purchased 67.897 shares. When you divide the $500 by the total number of shares purchased, you get an average of only $7.36 per share. Even though the price of the mutual fund fell 10% from the beginning of the analysis period to the end, the investor ends up with a 22% overall profit.

4. Plan of Action

If you don't have a plan to control conditions, you will be controlled by them. You must develop a plan and stick with it *no matter what.* Here are some creative ideas to help you implement your wealth-building program now.

1. **After paying the Lord's tithe, pay yourself next.**

   Depending upon your financial goals and the time availability to achieve them, after the Lord's tithe, dedicate at least 10% of your income to an investment program. Study the Rejoicing Tithe of Deuteronomy 14:22-26. The less money you feel you have for such a plan, the more vital it is to initiate this program. I know a man who calls this *his* personal income tax. He says that when he thinks of it as a tax, it gets paid. Nobody likes to pay tax but it does get paid.

   God will underwrite the initiation of your program to pay his tithe first and yourself second. He promises to give seed to the sower. (See Isaiah 55:10-11 and II Corinthians 9:10-11.)

   It is your duty to continue the program by doggedly avoiding the consumption of all your harvest. Sow the seed; eat only the bread. This is God's key to make you "rich" (II Corinthians 9:11) and fulfill the covenant of being blessed and being a blessing (Genesis 12:2).

2. **In your quest for seed, reduce your cost of living and invest the savings.**

   You can "create" investment capital by carefully reviewing the "299 Ways to Stretch Your Dollars" found in Section 7 of this text. Until your plan is fully initiated and under way, you may have to frugally economize or

Proverbs 21:5

The plans of the diligent lead to profit as surely as haste leads to poverty.

even do without many discretionary expense items such as spa memberships, cable TV, excessive eating out, etc.

Ask yourself, "Is it really wise to enjoy immediate gratification or would it be more prudent to postpone gratification of the moment for the long-term results of reaching my financial goal(s)?" "Am I eating my seed?"

3. **Dedicate any extra income.**

   Unexpected money, year-end bonuses, money you have found, money earned from overtime, a windfall inheritance or income from a small business undertaking can be dedicated to your plan.

4. **After you have paid off a loan, continue making the monthly payment to your investment program.**

5. **Avoid *overpaying* federal income taxes.**

   Judge Learned Hand said: "Anyone may so arrange their affairs so that their taxes are as low as possible. No one owes any public duty to pay more than the law demands."

   Become familiar with the tax laws. The tax laws don't harm you as much as what you don't know about them.

Matthew 22:21

Then He said to them, "Give to Caesar what is Caesar's, and to God what is God's."

Order and read the free book from the Internal Revenue Service known as Publication 17, *Your Federal Income Tax.*

Romans 13:6

This is also why you pay taxes, for the authorities are God's servants, who give their time to governing. Give everyone what you owe him: If you owe taxes, pay taxes.

LEGAL TAX-REDUCING STRATEGIES

1. **Start a small business.**

   - To be in business you must have a product or a service you regularly offer to the public with the intent to produce a profit.
   - As a business person, you will be eligible for 27 different tax deductions you do not otherwise qualify for as an individual. (See the 27 expense lines on a Schedule C.)
   - Call or write the IRS and ask them to send you a free book known as Publication 334, *A Tax Guide for Small Business.*
   - With a small business you may qualify for:

Proverbs 24:27

Finish your outdoor work and get your fields ready; after that, build your house.

Asset expensing (Section 179 assets)

You can take the assets that you are going to buy and use at least 51% of the time in your business, assets such as office equipment, copiers or computers, etc. and deduct the cost of them up to the amount given in IRS

Publication 334 directly off the top of your income.

Tax deductible travel

If a trip relates to your current job or occupation, it is deductible. You can deduct the cost of many business seminars, trade shows and conventions.

Office in your home

If you establish an identifiable portion of your home used regularly and exclusively for your business activity you may get a tax break. It must be your principal place of business or a meeting place for your customers or clients. Be sure and check with the IRS for the latest regulations.

Put your children to work in your business

Rather than doling out an allowance, teach responsibility to your children by putting them to work in your part-time business addressing envelopes, cleaning the office in the home or even washing the business car. You can easily justify a salary of up to $30 a week and claim it as a business deduction.

2. Consider giving creatively.

If you are wishing to put some monies aside for

college costs for your child, 14 or older, here is a strategy for you: if you have appreciated stock in your investment portfolio you wish to sell, and you know you will be facing a tax on the gain, give the stock to your child as a gift. A gift of up to $10,000 ($20,000 for a married couple) is tax-free to the child.

When your child sells the stock, tax will be levied at the child's rate. If your child is under 14, then the first $650 in his or her name is tax-free and the next $650 is taxed at the child's rate. Any unearned income over that is taxed at the parent's highest marginal rate.

3. Donate strategically.

If you give appreciated stock to your church, you pay no capital gain tax and you get to deduct the fair market value which includes the gain. Let the church then liquidate the stock.

4. Give yourself a tax-free raise.

- The government knows that the average person would never apply enough discipline to set aside money for taxes and pay them all at once on April 15. That is why taxes are deducted from your paycheck *before* you receive it. But over 100 million American taxpayers *overwithhold.* In so doing they are making an *interest-free* loan to Uncle Sam. Why give the government money to hold for you? Use that money in your plan instead.

- Go to your employer and obtain an IRS W-4 form. Use its accompanying worksheet to compute your withholding so at tax time, neither you nor the government owes one another. You may be able to increase your take-home pay by $100 or more. Don't spend it.

Invest it. You worked hard for the money, now let it work even harder for you in your investment program.

5. **Open an Individual Retirement Arrangement (IRA).**

- An IRA is an investment program for your retirement where money can compound and grow until withdrawal without the ravages of taxation. See the diagram on the next page to determine if your contributions can be tax deductible.

- Even if you don't qualify for a deductible contribution to an IRA, it is usually to your advantage to annually contribute non-deductible dollars to the maximum the law allows so the earnings can grow tax deferred.

- If you are self-employed or even if you moonlight and participate in a pension plan at your full-time job, you can open a Keogh Retirement Plan (HR-10) and each year you can contribute up to $30,000 or 15% (whichever is lesser) of your free-lance earnings to a tax-deferred retirement plan and that contribution is all deductible.

- Open your IRA where you can manage your own account—a self-directed account. Choose a mutual fund family that has no-load stock funds, no-load bond funds and a money market fund or consider an IRA with a discount broker such as Charles Schwab. Their program allows you to move among many fund families and follow the Money Movement Strategy described earlier.

Proverbs 10:8

Gather crops in summer.

When Is An IRA Contribution Tax Deductible?

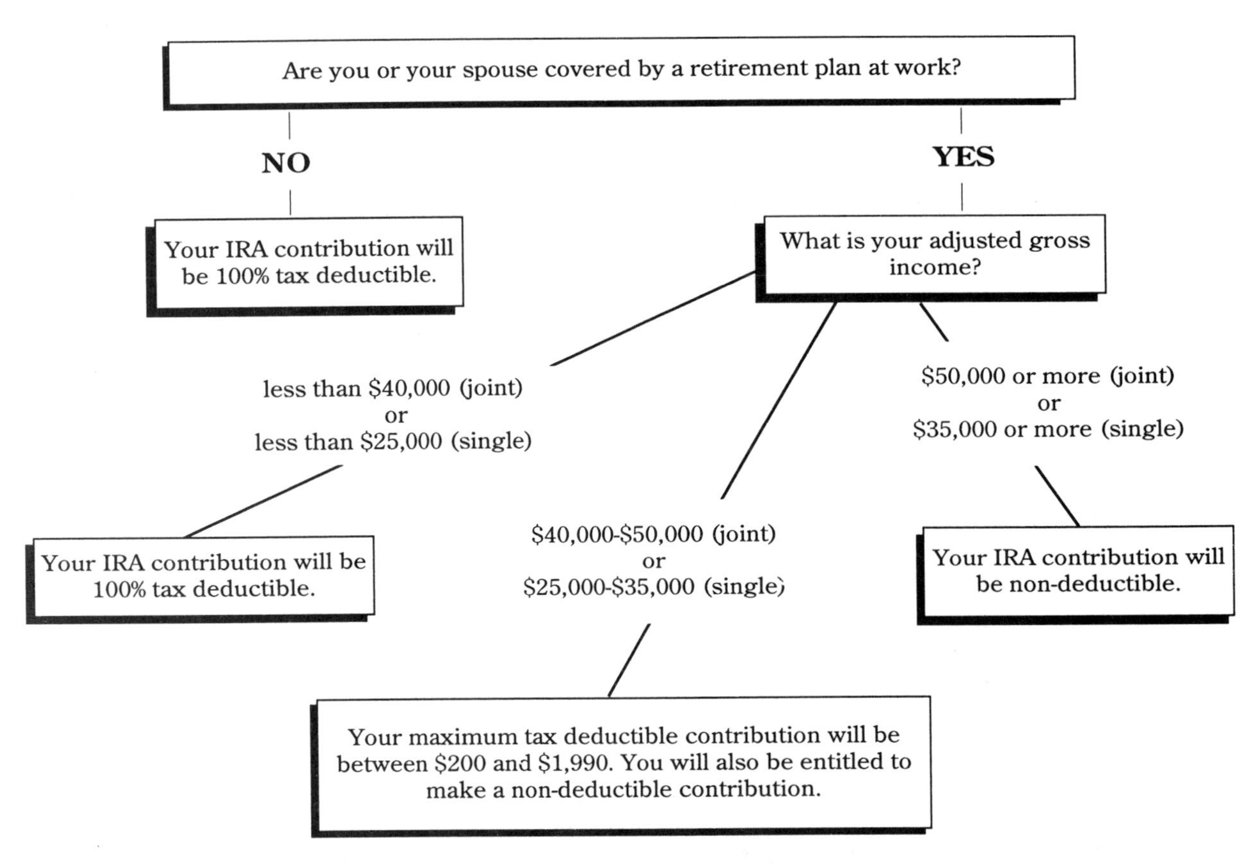

Example: A married couple, filing a joint return, has an adjusted gross income of $43,000. They both work and have IRAs. One spouse is an active participant in an employer-maintained retirement plan. Before 1987 each spouse could contribute and deduct $2,000 each or $4,000 but that is no longer the case. Now, because one spouse participates in a retirement plan, and their combined income falls within the $40,000 to $50,000 phaseout range, they cannot take a deduction for the full amount. They must apply the following formula:

1).	Regular deduction limit		$4,000
2).	Excess AGI amount ($43,000-$40,000)	$3,000	
3).	$10,000	10,000	
4).	Divide line 2 by line 3	0.3	
5).	Multiply line 1 by line 4 and round to the next highest multiple of $10		1,200
6)	Allowable deduction—line 1 minus line 5 If this amount is between $0 and $200, enter $200		$2,800

This $2,800 will then be allocated between husband and wife with neither one getting more than $2,000.

COMPARATIVE RATE OF RETURN WITH AND WITHOUT AN IRA

Imagine a 30-year-old wage earner in the 28% tax bracket. Assume that this worker contributed $2,000 per year ($166.66 monthly) until age 65. Compare the amounts accumulated with an IRA—and without.

	10%		12%	
Rate of Return	Without IRA	With IRA	Without IRA	With IRA
Annual contribution	$2,000	$2,000	$2,000	$2,000
Income taxes	$ 560	$ -0-	$ 560	$ -0-
Amount left to invest	$1,440	$2,000	$1,440	$2,000
Effective rate of interest	7.2%	10%	8.64%	12%
Total accumulation after 35 years	$226,707	$632,773	$322,529	$1,071,827

TITHE OF ALL INVESTMENT INCREASE

Any capital gain from the sale of an asset such as stocks or real estate is a "titheable" event. Don't forget to tithe on any matching fund contributions your employer makes to a 401(k) program on your behalf.

Rather than waiting until the final sale, ask God if you should pay tithe on reinvested dividends and interest on all compounding, liquid investments including tax-sheltered investments. An ideal time to pay this tithe would be when you receive your year-end statement showing interest and dividends.

It is a false rationalization to reason that keeping the tithe invested will make it grow to even more for the Lord when you finally sell. God expects his portion of the increase as a *firstfruit*. Besides in comparison, the 100-fold return (about 10,000%) is far greater than the measly growth your investment may yield!

II Chronicles 31:5

...a tithe of everything.

Matthew 13:23

The seed that fell on good soil...produces a crop, yielding a hundred, sixty or thirty times what was sown.

CHAPTER 9

MAKING BIBLICAL ECONOMICS WORK IN YOUR LIFE

In this course of study of biblical economics you have learned the truths Satan desperately wants to remain hidden. He wants wealth and power to continue to be in the hands of his people.

He shudders at the thought of Christians learning the following:

- The wealth of the world is really theirs

Proverbs 13:22

A sinners' wealth is stored up for the righteous.

- God has given to the sinner the task of storing wealth for the righteous

Ecclesiastes 2:26

To the sinner he gives the task of gathering and storing up wealth to hand it over to the one who pleases God.

- Unjust gain is ultimately to be turned over to the righteous

Proverbs 28:8 (KJV)

He that by usury and unjust gain increaseth his substance, he shall gather it for him that will pity the poor.

This inversion of wealth will not happen automatically. It will involve:

- Enforcing the return of what Satan has stolen

Matthew 11:12

From the days of John the Baptist until now, the kingdom of heaven has been forcefully advancing and forceful men lay hold of it.

- Standing your ground

I Timothy 6:12

Fight the good fight of faith.

Ephesians 6:13,14

After you have done everything to stand, stand firm then.

To insure an unshakable financial future, able to withstand the ups and downs of financial cycles and Satan's assaults, implement these steps:

1. Be committed to the Word of God

Luke 6:46-49

"Why do you call me, 'Lord, Lord,' and do not do what I say? I will show you what he is like who comes to me and <u>hears my words and puts them into practice</u>. He is like a man building a house, who dug down deep and laid the foundation on rock. *When* a flood came, the torrent struck that house but could not shake it, because it was well built. But the one who hears my words and does not put them into practice is like a man who built a house on the ground without a foundation. The moment the torrent struck that house, it collapsed and its destruction was complete."

2. Be aware that success is conditional upon positive action and faith.

John 13:17

Now that you know these things, you will be blessed *if* you do them.

3. Be consistent in your commitment to positive action.

James 1:25

But the man who looks intently into the perfect law that gives freedom, *and continues to do this*, not forgetting what he has heard, but

4. Be proactive, resolving to give the Lord some action to bless.

doing it—he will be blessed in what he *does*.

Joshua 1:8 (KJV)

This book of the law shall not depart out of thy mouth; but thou shalt meditate therein day and night that thou mayest observe to do according to all that is written therein; for then thou shalt make thy way prosperous, and then thou shalt have good success.

Psalm 1:1-3

Blessed is the man who does not walk in the counsel of the wicked or stand in the way of sinners or sit in the seat of mockers. But his delight is in the law of the Lord, and on his law he meditates day and night. He is like a tree planted by the streams of water, which yields its fruit in season and whose leaf does not wither. Whatever he *does* prospers.

INDEX OF SCRIPTURES

Money
and the
CHRISTIAN

Money
and the
CHRISTIAN

Money
and the
CHRISTIAN

NOTES:

NOTES:

ORDER FORM

ORDERED BY

Name ________________________
Please print clearly
Address ________________________
City ____________ State __ Zip ________
Telephone (___) __________
Daytime (___) __________

SHIP-TO ADDRESS

If different from "Ordered By" Address

Name ________________________
Address ________________________
City ____________ State __ Zip ________
Telephone (___) __________

ITEMS ORDERED

Note: Products purchased for professional purposes may be tax deductible.

Item	Price	Quantity	
***Money & the Christian* Syllabus**—The basic textbook for the seminar consisting of 9 sections and supporting material for the live, audio or video editions of the seminar	$20	____	________
Audio Tapes of *Money & the Christian* Seminar—10 audiocassette album of Caleb McAfee's seminar combining timeless biblical principles with timely money strategies	$49	____	________
Start Your Own Business—A Christian's step-by-step guide to successfully starting and operating a profitable business	$59	____	________
Home Free!—Kit contains a booklet and 2 audiocassettes on how you can have a debt-free home for the glory of God; includes a coupon for a free personalized mortgage analysis showing suggested rapid debt reduction strategies	$20	____	________
Video Edition—10 sessions of the *Money and the Christian* seminar with Caleb McAfee on 5 videos; suitable for group presentations; includes one *Money & the Christian* syllabus	$195	____	________

SUBTOTAL FROM ABOVE .... ________

Sales tax (Texas residents, please add 8.25%) .... ________

Shipping and handling ($6 for first item, $2 for each additional item sent to same address) .... ________

For shipments outside USA, add $7 to above shipping/handling and pay in U.S. funds .... ________

Contribution to help the McAfees in the work of the ministry (tax deductible) .... ________

TOTAL ENCLOSED .... ________

Thank you for your order!

METHOD OF PAYMENT

☐ Enclosed is my check or money order made payable to **Money and the Christian.**

☐ Please charge to: ☐ MasterCard ☐ Visa

Credit card account number

Exp. Date ___/___ Signature ________________________

SEND YOUR ORDER TO

Money and the Christian
P.O. Box 153989
Irving, Texas 75015-3989

Telephone (972) 438-1234

Prices subject to change.

ORDER FORM

ORDERED BY

Name______________________________
Please print clearly
Address______________________________
City ______________ State ___ Zip __________
Telephone (___) ____________
Daytime (___) ____________

SHIP-TO ADDRESS

If different from "Ordered By" Address

Name______________________________
Address______________________________
City ______________ State __ Zip__________
Telephone (___) ______________

ITEMS ORDERED

Note: Products purchased for professional purposes may be tax deductible.

		Quantity	
***Money & the Christian* Syllabus**—The basic textbook for the seminar consisting of 9 sections and supporting material for the live, audio or video editions of the seminar	$20	____	________
Audio Tapes of *Money & the Christian* Seminar—10 audiocassette album of Caleb McAfee's seminar combining timeless biblical principles with timely money strategies	$49	____	________
Start Your Own Business—A Christian's step-by-step guide to successfully starting and operating a profitable business	$59	____	________
Home Free!—Kit contains a booklet and 2 audiocassettes on how you can have a debt-free home for the glory of God; includes a coupon for a free personalized mortgage analysis showing suggested rapid debt reduction strategies	$20	____	________
Video Edition—10 sessions of the *Money and the Christian* seminar with Caleb McAfee on 5 videos; suitable for group presentations; includes one *Money & the Christian* syllabus	$195	____	________
SUBTOTAL FROM ABOVE			________
Sales tax (Texas residents, please add 8.25%)			________
Shipping and handling ($6 for first item, $2 for each additional item sent to same address)			________
For shipments outside USA, add $7 to above shipping/handling and pay in U.S. funds			________
Contribution to help the McAfees in the work of the ministry (tax deductible)			________
TOTAL ENCLOSED			________

Thank you for your order!

METHOD OF PAYMENT

☐ Enclosed is my check or money order made payable to **Money and the Christian.**

☐ Please charge to: ☐ MasterCard ☐ Visa

Credit card account number

Exp. Date ___/___ Signature ____________________

SEND YOUR ORDER TO

Money and the Christian
P.O. Box 153989
Irving, Texas 75015-3989

Telephone (972) 438-1234

Prices subject to change.